W9-BCN-826

TONYDUNGY

Read all of the books in this exciting, action-packed biography series!

For my not-so-little Little Brother, Matt

Copyright © 2009 by Lerner Publishing Group, Inc.

Sports Heroes and Legends™ is a trademark of Barnes and Noble, Inc.

Used with permission from Barnes and Noble, Inc.

Twenty-First Century Books
A division of Lerner Publishing Group, Inc.
241 First Avenue North
Minneapolis, MN 55401 U.S.A.

Website address: www.lernerbooks.com

Front Cover: Jed Jacobsohn/Getty Images
Front Cover Background: © Kenneth Garrett/National Geographic/Getty Images
Back Cover: © iStockphoto.com/John Mansfield

Library of Congress Cataloging-in-Publication Data

Doeden, Matt.
   Tony Dungy / by Matt Doeden.
      p.   cm. — (Sports heroes and legends)
   Includes bibliographical references and index.
      ISBN: 978-0-7613-4225-0 (lib. bdg. : alk. paper) 1. Dungy, Tony—Juvenile
literature. 2. Football coaches—United States—Biography—Juvenile literature.
3. African American football coaches—Biography—Juvenile literature. I. Title.
   GV939.D84D63 2009
   796.332092—dc22 [B]   2008051329

Manufactured in the United States of America
1 2 3 4 5 6 – JR – 14 13 12 11 10 09

Sports Heroes
and LEGENDS™

TONY DUNGY

by Matt Doeden

TFCB Twenty-First Century Books/Minneapolis

Contents

Breaking into the Win Column

Zero wins, five losses. That was the record forty-one-year-old Tony Dungy had built up with the Tampa Bay Buccaneers in his brief time as a National Football League (NFL) head coach. Few fans expected Tony to finally notch his first victory on October 13, 1996, when the Bucs were playing host to the Minnesota Vikings. The Vikings owned the NFL's best record at 5–1. And as if that wasn't enough, the Vikings were Tony's old team. He'd spent four years there as defensive coordinator until, after the 1995 season, he took the Tampa Bay head-coaching job.

"Coach didn't look like he was sleeping too well," said Tampa defensive tackle Warren Sapp about Tony before the game. "His hair wasn't cut. He looked tired. We wanted to go out and win one for him."

Before the game, Tony greeted Minnesota head coach Dennis Green—his former boss—and many of his former players.

Despite the Vikings' great record, Tony remained confident that his team was up to the challenge.

At first, it looked as if there was little reason to hold on to that confidence. The Vikings drove down the field and scored a touchdown on a 26-yard run by running back Robert Smith. In the second quarter, Tampa's offense, led by quarterback Trent Dilfer, put together a 17-play drive that took them deep into Viking territory. Kicker Michael Husted came onto the field for what should have been an easy 31-yard field goal attempt. But it seemed that the Bucs' losing ways would continue when Husted missed the kick.

At halftime, Tony was busy making adjustments to his game plan. He knew the Vikings inside and out, and he saw some ways to beat them—including a heavier reliance on the passing attack. Tony's new plan worked perfectly. The Bucs came out looking like a different team. Dilfer connected with receiver Robb Thomas for a 31-yard touchdown to tie the game. After the Vikings reclaimed the lead with a field goal, Tampa fullback Mike Alstott caught a pass and rammed through Viking defenders into the end zone for a 12-yard score. The Bucs never looked back, adding another Thomas touchdown and harassing Viking quarterback Warren Moon throughout the second half.

Late in the game, with the Vikings attempting a late comeback, Sapp burst through Minnesota's offensive line and leveled Moon, causing a fumble. Tampa's Chidi Ahanotu fell on the ball for the recovery, and the game was all but over. The Buccaneers held on for a shocking 24–13 victory, finally breaking into the win column. Tony had done it! It was his first win as an NFL head coach. In celebration, his players doused him with Gatorade—a tradition in the NFL for big victories.

"We are really excited," Dungy said of his team. "It was a win we needed badly. And to get it against the Vikings makes it special because the Vikings are a great football team."

It was just one win in a long season. But it was enough to give the Buccaneers hope. And it showed that Tony had what it took to win as an NFL head coach.

Chapter One

Student and Athlete

Anthony Kevin Dungy was born October 6, 1955, in Jackson, Michigan. The second of Wilbur and CleoMae Dungy's four children, Tony understood the importance of education from an early age. His dad was a physiology professor at a local community college and his mom taught high school English. Tony, his brother, Linden, and sisters, Sherrie and Lauren, were expected to study hard and get good grades.

> Tony's brother, Linden, is a dentist with his own practice. His sister Sherrie is a nurse, and Lauren is a doctor who cares for women with high-risk pregnancies.

Tony later credited his parents with instilling his famous work ethic, love for learning, and confidence. "Our parents encouraged us to follow our dreams and told us that if we wanted to do something, we could do it," he wrote in his auto-biography, *Quiet Strength*.

Tony also got his natural athleticism and love of sports from his parents—especially his mother. CleoMae had been a star basketball player in her youth. Wilbur had been a champion boxer and had competed in track and field.

In his autobiography, Tony admits that he couldn't beat his mother in a footrace until he was in the seventh grade.

In 1963 Wilbur and CleoMae enrolled at Michigan State University (MSU) to continue their educations. They moved the family to nearby East Lansing, Michigan. Tony became fasci-nated with the MSU Spartans football team, coached by Duffy Daughtery. From an early age, Tony was a student of the game. His dad would often be studying while a game was on, but Tony made sure Wilbur followed the action.

Football wasn't the only sport that Tony loved. Basketball was another passion. He spent all the time he could on the basketball court, often playing against kids much older than himself. In fact, he frequently got into trouble for staying out past his curfew to play basketball.

The Dungys returned to Jackson in 1966. Tony went on to attend Parkside High School (his mother taught at rival Jackson High). Tony was an excellent student and a gifted athlete, and he was popular with his classmates. When he was fourteen, he was elected class president. He was on the baseball and track teams but really excelled in basketball and football. By tenth grade, he was Parkside's starting quarterback and a star guard on the basketball team. Already, he was dreaming of a future playing football for Daughtery and his beloved MSU Spartans.

In 1971, Tony's junior year, he and receiver Bobby Burton led Parkside's football team to an 8–1 record. The two made a lethal combination on the field, connecting for four touchdowns in one game. After the season, the coaches held an annual banquet for the players. Part of the banquet was the announcement of the following year's captains. The coaches announced three captains, and Tony was one of them. But Tony was furious. He'd been named, but Burton had not. Tony believed that the coaches had not wanted to name more than one black captain (the school was predominantly white). Angrily, Tony told the coach that he was quitting the team.

Many of the other players saw Tony as a leader. Burton and several others vowed to stand by him and sit out their senior seasons. The other two boys who had been named captains vowed to decline the honor.

"I don't think people thought someone at that age would have enough guts to . . . say 'You know this is totally wrong, and I'm not going to play this game with you,'" Burton later said. "It showed [Tony] was willing to take risks and . . . deal with the outcome."

BLOWING HIS TOP

Tony is famous for his calm, unflappable demeanor. But he wasn't always that way. In a ninth-grade basketball game, his temper got the best of him. He was angry that the other team was treating him roughly. He believed he was getting fouled on play after play, but the officials weren't blowing the whistle. Finally, he'd had enough. After yet another play where he thought he'd been fouled, he hauled off and punched the offending player.

"It looked just like a cartoon," recalled Tony's friend and teammate Bobby Burton. "The kid hit the floor and started sliding back. It was one of those youthful things. That was the one and only time. Tony was normally the person we looked up to."

Tony was prepared to focus on basketball. He believed that he had a better chance at a basketball scholarship anyway. But before his senior year, a guidance counselor pulled Tony aside and talked him out of quitting the football team. Reluctantly, Tony and his friends rejoined the team.

It turned out to be an excellent decision. Tony led Parkside to an 8–2 season in 1972. He completed 91 of 167 passes for 1,467 yards and 24 touchdowns. He was named to the Class A All-State team. He also earned All-State honors on the basketball team (he was Parkside's leading scorer) and the baseball team (he was a pitcher and an infielder).

❝*The most appealing thing about Tony is that he's not going to shortchange you on anything. He's always been down to earth, a person that you liked. And it didn't take long to find that out.*❞

—BOBBY BURTON

Tony's natural athletic ability, combined with his good grades and intelligence, had attracted the attention of college scouts. But his dream of playing for Daughtery at MSU had disappeared when the legendary coach retired after the 1972 season. So Tony considered a wide range of schools. He could play basketball at Duke or Arizona or play football at the University of Southern California (USC). But as time passed, one school stood out for seventeen-year-old Tony—the University of Minnesota. Minnesota had everything Tony wanted. Second-year head coach Cal Stoll had been an assistant under Daughtery at MSU—and like MSU, Minnesota was in the Big Ten conference. So Tony thought it was about as close as he could come to his dream. Stoll had no problems with playing a black quarterback, which was unusual for coaches at the time. Another plus was that at Minnesota, Tony could play for both the football and basketball teams, an option not available at most other schools. Minnesota also had good economics and business programs, which were the subjects that most interested Tony.

"I took a [recruiting] trip to Minnesota and looked around the Twin Cities and fell in love with the area," Tony later said. All of these factors made Tony's decision easy. He announced that he was going to become a Minnesota Golden Gopher.

Chapter Two

College Quarterback

Tony arrived at the University of Minnesota campus in Minneapolis in late summer of 1973 to begin practice with the football team. Tony seemed like a perfect fit for Stoll's "Veer-T" offense, which heavily featured a running quarterback (though sophomore John Lawing would begin the season with the starting quarterback job). The Gopher coaches stressed hard work and determination, ideas that resonated with Tony.

"Success is uncommon and not to be enjoyed by the common man," Stoll told his players. "I'm looking for uncommon people because we want to be successful, not average."

Stoll was a great motivator. His players were fired up and ready to go for the season opener against powerhouse Ohio State, which was ranked third in the nation. Their enthusiasm was quickly dampened, however, by a 56–7 thrashing at the hands of the Buckeyes. Tony played only briefly at the end of the game, long after the outcome had been determined. But Tony saw some meaningful playing time the following week. The Gophers played North Dakota in Minnesota's home opener. Stoll put Tony into the game in the second half, after the Minnesota defense had intercepted a pass deep in North Dakota territory. Tony got the snap and took off running. He broke three tackles as he darted into the end zone for his first college touchdown. The score helped seal a 41–14 Gopher victory.

Veer-T

The Veer-T offense that Stoll used in Minnesota was built on running the ball with the quarterback and two split running backs. The two running backs stood behind the quarterback, forming a T shape. The option play was heavily featured in the offense. In the option, the quarterback rolls to one side with the ball and looks at the defense. If the defense pursues the quarterback, he flips the ball to the running back on that side (while the other running back becomes a blocker). If the defense covers the running back, the quarterback keeps the ball and rushes it himself.

Two weeks later, on his eighteenth birthday, Tony got his first college start. Lawing had been injured during a loss to

Kansas the previous week, which meant that Tony would play in front of a full house at Minnesota's Memorial Stadium. The Gophers were playing the Nebraska Cornhuskers, the number two team in the nation. Knowing that the Gophers couldn't stack up to Nebraska in talent, Stoll decided to try a grinding running attack, with Tony as his main weapon. So Tony ran the ball on play after play—on 15 of Minnesota's first 19 plays, in fact. Tony was running the option, but the Nebraska defense was homing in on the Minnesota running backs, preventing Tony from giving up the ball.

"They wouldn't let me pitch it," Tony said. "So I kept the ball myself. The keeper was the only option they gave me."

Nebraska fumbled on its first drive, and Tony and the offense quickly responded. Tony scampered 10 yards to the end zone and gave the Gophers a surprising 7–0 lead. But the good feelings didn't last long. Nebraska took over the game, scoring at will and shutting down the Minnesota offense in a 48–7 victory.

Against Iowa two weeks later, Tony came into the game for Lawing in the second half. He looked bad at first, however. "I was having trouble with my timing because the Iowa defense was jumping around and I was trying to wait for them before I called my plays," he said. "We weren't running smooth." But Tony and the offense got it together in the fourth quarter. Tony's 5-yard touchdown run sealed a 31–23 Minnesota victory.

66*About the middle of my freshman year, I started to have my doubts [about being able to play effectively]. I didn't know if I'd ever be good enough. People were starting to say I couldn't play or that the Gophers couldn't win until they got a different quarterback. But Coach Stoll kept faith in me.*99

—TONY DUNGY

Tony didn't play much for the rest of the season. He ended it having completed just 8 of 33 pass attempts for 97 yards and 1 touchdown, and added 156 rushing yards. A season-ending four-game winning streak led the Gophers to finish 7–4 (6–2 in the Big Ten conference, good for third place). All told, it had been a pretty good season. The Gophers had played well, and Tony had gotten a good taste of what it took to be a college quarterback. After the football season, Tony's attention turned to basketball. He was a guard on the Gopher team that finished 12–12 (6–8 in the Big Ten), although he didn't see much playing time. He played in sixteen games, averaging just 2.6 points and one rebound per game. Tony also focused on his studies in economics.

> **❝**You can't look at someone on your own team as competition because you're both out there working for the same goal. If you do start thinking that way, it's all over because the guy who isn't thinking that way will win the [starting] job. You can't let the situation pressure you.**❞**
>
> —JOHN LAWING ON THE COMPETITION FOR THE STARTING QUARTERBACK JOB IN 1973

After the 1973 season, Lawing left Minnesota and transferred to North Carolina. That left eighteen-year-old Tony as the Gophers' starting quarterback. Tony was confident, both in himself and in his team.

"Last year, 99 out of 100 times I would run exactly the play [the coaches] gave me because I didn't really feel confident [changing it]," he said. "This year . . . I've called a lot of them at the line myself. . . . The only goal we can have is to win. . . . I want to win every game we play."

Stoll shared Tony's confidence. "Dungy is going to be a great quarterback," said the coach. "He's very bright and one of the most dedicated athletes I've coached. He watches game films so much you have to turn off the lights and kick him out of the building. The thing that scares me is he's smarter than I am."

Once again, the Gophers opened the season against Ohio State (ranked fourth in the nation). And once again the Buckeyes won the game. But this time, the Gophers were more competitive and kept the game close right up to the end. In spite of the final score of 34–19, Tony and his teammates felt confident after the contest.

"We proved to ourselves that we're a team that won't give up, even if it's 99–0," Tony said of the effort.

The team's second game, against North Dakota, started out rough. Tony fumbled on the second play of the game, contributing to an early 10–0 deficit. But Tony and the Gophers bounced back, scoring four times before the end of the half to take control. Tony started the comeback with a 9-yard touchdown pass to tight end Scott Puchtel. Then he hit running back Rick Upchurch with two touchdown passes before running in an 8-yard score of his own. Tony added another touchdown pass to Upchurch later and tied a school record with 4 touchdown passes in a single game. Tony also ran for 149 yards in the 42–30 Gopher win. All the running had taken a toll on his body, however, and he had badly bruised his throwing shoulder.

The injury slowed down Tony in the next game, against Texas Christian University (TCU). The Gophers were expected to win handily. But Tony didn't play well, possibly because of the injury, and Minnesota squeaked by with a 9–7 victory.

The aching shoulder, along with a knee injury, plagued Tony for the rest of the season. He had to miss some games, including a 54–0 crushing at the hands of Nebraska.

Tony and the Gophers bounced back on October 19 against the Iowa Hawkeyes. On their first offensive play, Tony pitched the ball to Upchurch for an 86-yard touchdown run. The strong running game and a punishing effort from the defense gave the Gophers a much-needed 23–17 victory.

"It was kind of a do-or-die situation for us," Tony admitted. "We needed [a win] to be ready mentally before we go and play Michigan next week. We're heading back uphill now."

The momentum gained in the Iowa win didn't last long. Michigan easily handled the Gophers in a 49–0 blowout the following week, and then Minnesota lost 21–13 to Northwestern, falling to 3–5 for the season.

The team got only one more win the rest of the season, 24–20 against Purdue. But even that victory came with bad news. Tony badly sprained his ankle in the third quarter and had to leave the game. The next week, the Gophers blew a lead late in the game to lose to Illinois, and they wrapped up the season by suffering a blowout at the hands of Wisconsin. Their final record of 4–7 (2–6 in the Big Ten) was a bitter disappointment. Over the course of the season, Tony had completed 39 of 94 passes for 612 yards and 5 touchdowns.

THE LITTLE EIGHT

The Big Ten conference included ten teams until Penn State joined in 1990. For years, the conference was almost always dominated by two powerhouses—Ohio State and Michigan. For that reason, fans and media often referred to those two schools as the Big Two and the other eight schools in the conference, including the Gophers, as the Little Eight. Often, third place in the Big Ten was the best finish that most of these teams could reasonably hope to achieve.

Tony's body was still battered and bruised after the season ended. So he decided that it was time to give up basketball. By leaving the basketball team, he could have more time to heal, and he could also spend more time focusing on his studies. Playing two sports and balancing a full class load was, according to Tony, "more than I could handle."

Tony and his teammates entered the 1975 season looking for improvement. Stoll had abandoned the old Veer-T offense, favoring instead a more aerial attack. Minnesota started out with a 20–14 loss to Indiana but bounced back with a 38–0 win over Western Michigan (a game for which Tony was named United Press International's Back of the

Week). Tony played poorly in the third game, against Oregon, but the Gophers still managed to pull out a 10–7 victory. Tony played much better the next week against Ohio University. His 38-yard touchdown pass to Mike Jones was the highlight of a 21–0 Gopher win.

Tony explained how the touchdown play had worked. "That was a read-route play-action pass. [Jones] is supposed to read the defender; he could have either curled out or run the post (straight route) like he did. Luckily I was able to read his pattern and get the ball to him."

Tony had his best game of the early season against Illinois. He completed 14 of 31 passes for 216 yards and 3 touchdowns. But it wasn't enough to win the game. The Minnesota defense couldn't handle the Illinois attack, and the Gophers lost, 42–23. Another loss, 38–15 to Michigan State, dropped the Gophers to 3–3 for the season and 0–3 in the Big Ten.

The Gophers finally scored their first Big Ten win the next week against Iowa. Tony played well again, handing the ball off, running, and completing short, safe passes as the Gophers earned a 31–7 victory.

The win set up a showdown with the powerful Michigan Wolverines, ranked seventh in the nation. The Gophers, heavy underdogs in the game, came out firing. Tony completed 12 of 16 passes in the first half, including two touchdowns. They were his ninth and tenth touchdown passes of the year, breaking the school's single-season record of 9. His efforts kept the Gophers in the game, down 21–14 at halftime. Minnesota gave Michigan a scare in the second half, scoring again to tie it at 21 and igniting the Gopher crowd. But in the end, Michigan proved too strong and managed a tight 28–21 victory. It was another loss, but this time the Gophers could feel good about their play.

"We know we can play with the big boys," Stoll said after the game. "Now we just have to find out how to beat them."

Tony had one of his finest games as a Gopher on November 6 against Northwestern. It was a matchup of the Big Ten's top two passers, Tony and Northwestern's Randy Dean, and Tony came out on top. He threw 4 touchdown passes in Minnesota's 33–9 victory, matching his own school record. One of his touchdowns went to Jones on a spectacular diving catch. Tony also set a school record for career touchdown passes during the game. His first touchdown was the seventeenth of his career, breaking the old mark of sixteen held by John Hankenson.

Tony deflected the praise that came his way after the game. "Those guys were catching everything," he said. "My receivers are my bread and butter. They make me look awfully good."

Next up was Ohio State, the number one team in the nation, and another chance for Stoll's Gophers to prove themselves against some of the Big Ten's "big boys." Before the game, Buckeye defensive coordinator George Hill heaped praise on Tony and the Minnesota offense. "In Minnesota and Dungy, we're going to run into the best passing team we've faced," he said. "We've seen some good passing teams . . . but none of them had people who could do things like Dungy can do."

Hill's defense was ready, however, and proved why the Buckeyes were the best team in the nation. The Ohio State defense swarmed all over the field, frustrating and confusing Tony and the offense. In the first half, Tony didn't complete any of his five pass attempts, and two of them were intercepted. The second half was a little better, and Tony's 5-yard touchdown pass to fullback Greg Barlow accounted for the only Gopher points. But it wasn't nearly enough, and Ohio State cruised to a 38–6 victory.

"It was a combination of their [pass] rush, my not throwing real well, and their pass coverage," Tony explained. "You know some days you have it and some days you don't, and today I didn't have it."

The 5–5 Gophers hosted the Wisconsin Badgers in the final game of the season, needing a victory to finish the season with a winning record. The team was up to the task, with Tony leading the way. He led three touchdown drives—scoring two rushing touchdowns himself—on the way to an impressive 24–3 victory. Tony also threw his fifteenth touchdown pass of the season, a Big Ten record.

The Gophers finished the season 6–5, though just 3–5 in the Big Ten. Despite the disappointing record, Tony had enjoyed a brilliant season. He had completed 123 of 225 passes for 1,515 yards and 15 touchdowns and added 244 yards rushing. His 1,759 yards of total offense (the total sum of passing yards, rushing yards, and receiving yards) ranked fifth in the nation. He was named Minnesota's most valuable player (MVP) and earned second-team All–Big Ten honors (meaning he was chosen as the Big Ten conference's second-best quarterback).

Chapter | Three

Senior Leader

Tony, his teammates, and many Gopher fans looked ahead to the 1976 season with optimism. "We've worked our tails off the last few years to gain respectability," Tony, the team captain, said. "I believe we gained just that the last half of 1975. We finally began to play the kind of football we want, the coaches want, and our fans want. This year we have the deepest, most experienced team Coach Stoll has put together since his first season in 1972. We know we are winners. We know we can do it. All we need for help is our share of the breaks and a lot of good health."

The Gophers started out with a bang against Indiana in the season opener. They opened the scoring on a blocked punt, and then Tony led the team on two touchdown drives, running for both scores himself. The Gophers took a 19–0 lead into halftime and looked to put the game out of reach in the third quarter.

"We figured if we could control the ball at the start of the third quarter, we could keep our momentum," Tony said.

❝Once we get a couple wins under our belts and put it all together, there is no telling how far we can go. We all have our own dreams, but I can tell you now each of us is dreaming of some mighty big wins this fall. . . . Now all we have to do is make those dreams a reality.❞

—TONY ON HIS HOPES FOR THE 1976 SEASON

The offense did exactly that. They took the opening kickoff and maintained a long, grinding drive that ate up time and culminated in a 15-yard touchdown pass from Tony to Ron Kullas. A late rally from Indiana was much too little, too late, and the Gophers held on for an impressive 32–13 win. For his efforts, Tony was named United Press International's Back of the Week.

Tony's good play continued in a 28–14 win over Washington State that moved the Gophers' record to 2–0. He completed 11 of 24 passes for 144 yards and added 62 rushing yards in the victory. The highlight of the game came in the second quarter, when Tony ran 51 yards for a touchdown—a play he described as "the longest run of my life."

The winning streak continued against Western Michigan, 21–10, though Tony struggled in the game. He completed just 3 of 14 first-half passes and threw two interceptions. The game remained in doubt right up to the end. In the final minute of play, Tony led a Minnesota drive and ran for the game-clinching touchdown, moving the Gophers to a perfect 3–0 for the year.

"I don't think there was one person in the huddle who thought we wouldn't win," Tony said of the final drive. "There wasn't any yelling or anything like that. We knew we had to score on that drive and that's all we thought about."

The shaky play against Western Michigan showed, however, that the Gophers weren't ready for the big time. They suffered their first loss of the season the following week, 38–7, against the underdog Washington Huskies.

Tony took it upon himself to get the team back on track on October 9 against Illinois. He had one of his best games as a Gopher, methodically dissecting the Illinois defense both on the ground and in the air. His final stats didn't look that impressive—just 76 yards in the air and 89 on the ground—but Stoll explained that stats didn't tell the whole story.

"[Tony's] statistics are something of record," Stoll explained. "But we as coaches can see how his mind is working, how he just picked apart the Illinois defense. He was unbelievable."

> **❝***Tony's real strengths are his intangibles. He has great leadership ability. He's the brightest young man I've coached. He's an All-American man as well as an All-American player.***❞**
>
> —CAL STOLL BEFORE THE 1976 SEASON

Tony was more reserved in talking about his own play. "It's not me at all," he said. "Our blocking was great. I think I'm just an average passer, but with all that time, anybody could do it."

The Gophers improved their Big Ten record to 3–0 (and their overall record to 5–1) with a win over Tony's old favorite team, Michigan State. The Gophers won in a defensive struggle, 14–10. Tony didn't have his best game, but his 9–15 performance (9 completions in 15 pass attempts) and 162 passing yards was enough. The disappointing loss to Washington earlier in the year was all but forgotten. Gopher fans started to wonder whether Tony could lead the team to a Big Ten title.

The Gophers traveled to Iowa to face the undermanned Hawkeyes. Most fans saw the game as little more than a warm-up for the following week's game against number-one-ranked Michigan. After a disappointing start, Minnesota jumped out to a 12–0 halftime lead. But they came out flat in the second half. Tony didn't look sharp, and his receivers were dropping passes. The Gopher defense fell apart completely. Iowa scored 22 unanswered points to hand the Gophers a shocking 22–12 loss. Just like that, hopes of a Big Ten title had all but died.

The shell-shocked Gophers looked even worse the next week against Michigan. A national television audience watched the Wolverines dominate the Gophers in every phase of the game. Michigan scored on six of its first seven possessions, while Tony and the Gopher offense couldn't manage any kind of attack against the Michigan defense. The result was an embarrassing 45–0 loss.

WORKING MAN

Tony had a number of jobs while in college to help pay for his living expenses. He worked at a meatpacking plant, on a farm, in a retail sporting goods store, and at the offices of General Mills, a food company based in Minnesota.

The Gophers bounced back with a 38–10 win over Northwestern, but it was their last real highlight of the season. They played a tough, defensive battle with eighth-ranked Ohio State but lost 9–3, then finished the season with a 26–17 loss to Wisconsin. In Tony's final game as a Gopher, he completed just 9 of 22 passes for 150 yards.

After such a promising start, the end of the Gophers' season was a bitter disappointment. They finished with a 6–5 record (4–4 in the Big Ten). Tony had enjoyed a great season individually, however. He completed 104 of 234 passes for 1,291 yards, though he had just four passing touchdowns. Once again, he was the team's MVP and a second-team All–Big Ten selection. He also received the Big Ten Medal of Honor for his combined athletic and academic achievements.

Tony finished his college career with a total of 3,515 passing yards and 1,165 rushing yards. His 4,680 yards of total offense was a Minnesota record and was fourth all time in the Big Ten. Additionally, he was Minnesota's all-time leading passer and leading rusher among quarterbacks. And his dedication to his studies had earned him a degree in business administration.

&&*I'm already richer than most people, considering all the breaks I have received, the fine people I live and work with, and being given the opportunity to gain a fine education playing the game I love. Yes, I'm pretty rich right now.*&&

—TONY ON HIS IDEA OF TRUE WEALTH

After such a successful college career, Tony looked ahead to the NFL. He played in several college all-star games early in

1977, including the East-West Shriners Game, the Hula Bowl, and the Japan Bowl. The games provided opportunities for NFL scouts to see college players and plan for the spring NFL draft.

Tony worked out for several teams, including the Washington Redskins. He hoped his workouts would impress the coaching staffs of these teams and help his draft position. Some people compared his quarterbacking style to Viking great Fran Tarkenton. With comparisons like that, Tony believed his future as an NFL quarterback was all but assured. He and roommate Mike Jones waited in their apartment for two days while the NFL draft took place. Both men waited for the phone to ring, eager to find out whether they'd been drafted. The NFL draft wasn't on television as it is today, so players were notified via telephone.

Tony and Jones waited by the phone through the entire first day of the draft. It never rang. But that was okay—they were confident they'd be selected in the late rounds on the second day. The next morning, they waited again. The phone finally rang that afternoon. It was the New York Giants, and they'd made their selection in the tenth round. But it wasn't Tony—they'd picked Jones.

Tony celebrated with his friend, then went back to waiting. He knew that only two rounds remained, but he was still confident he'd be drafted. He kept waiting. The afternoon turned into evening and the phone still hadn't rung. Eventually, Tony called a friend who worked for the Associated Press.

"Is the draft over?" he asked.

"Yeah, it's over," was the answer. Twelve rounds had come and gone, and nobody had drafted Tony. He had done a lot at the University of Minnesota, but apparently not enough. That evening, twenty-one-year-old Tony must have been wondering what direction his life would take.

Chapter Four

The NFL

Tony's disappointment in the NFL draft wasn't the end of the road for him in professional football. He still had plenty of opportunities ahead of him and choices to make. Many football experts thought Tony's quarterbacking style was a good fit for the Canadian Football League, which features a wider field that rewards running quarterbacks. The league's Montreal Alouettes wanted Tony to join their team.

"Keep your mind open to coming here," said Montreal coach Marv Levy. "You'd be perfect for this game with your style. You'll be in this league for a long time."

Tony was glad to have choices, but he dreamed of playing quarterback in the NFL. Several teams called and offered free-agent contracts. But to Tony's great disappointment, none of those teams wanted to sign him as a quarterback. They said that at 6 feet and 180 pounds, he wasn't big enough to play quarterback in the NFL. Instead, they wanted to convert him to safety, cornerback, or wide receiver.

Tony had a big decision to make. Montreal wanted him badly and offered him a $50,000 signing bonus to play quarterback. The Pittsburgh Steelers, meanwhile, were offering just a $2,200 bonus, and there was no guarantee he'd even make the team after completing training camp.

It was a tough decision, but Tony followed his heart. "I had always set my sights on the NFL," he later wrote. "I wanted to compete against the players I felt were the very best."

So Tony signed with Pittsburgh, one of the NFL's best teams. Led by head coach Chuck Noll, the Steelers had won Super Bowls after the 1974 and 1975 seasons. At first, Noll planned to convert Tony into a wide receiver. Former Gopher coach Tom Moore was the Steelers' wide receivers coach, so the move made sense. Tony reported to the team's training camp late in the summer of 1977. For two weeks, he practiced with the team's wide receivers, trying to learn the new position. But then injuries to the defensive backfield (cornerbacks and safeties) caused Noll to switch Tony to safety. Once again, Tony had to start learning a new position.

As a former quarterback, Tony understood the importance of study. He knew that he didn't have the physical gifts of some of the other defensive backs in camp. He also couldn't draw on years of experience playing the position. So he planned to

31

overcome those factors with preparation. He spent so much time watching game films that the coaches let him borrow a film projector so he could study in the evenings.

Meanwhile, Tony was forming close bonds with his team-mates. His parents had instilled a deep religious faith in him as a child, and he rediscovered that faith as a Steeler. Many of the team's players were devout Christians, and Tony fit right in.

As camp drew to a close, one big question remained: Would Tony make the team? As an undrafted free agent on a veteran team, the odds were stacked against him. But he survived one set of cuts after another. The weekend before the final cut, a Pittsburgh reporter wrote a story indicating which players the Steelers would cut. Tony's name was on the list. Dejected, Tony waited by the phone all weekend for the dreaded call. But just as his phone hadn't rung in the late rounds of the NFL draft, it didn't ring that weekend. He showed up for practice on Monday, still fearing a cut. But it never happened. Tony had made the team as a reserve safety!

When Tony made the Steelers' opening-day roster in 1977, he became the first undrafted free agent to make the team in two years.

The season started September 19. Tony's first game was a 19–0 win over the San Francisco 49ers. As a backup, his playing time was limited. But his solid play earned him more and more time on the field as the year went on. Most of that time was spent as a safety, but there was one notable exception. On October 9, the Steelers traveled to Houston to play the Oilers. As usual, Tony played safety. He even intercepted a Houston pass early in the game. As the game progressed, however, starting quarterback Terry Bradshaw was injured. In the fourth quarter, backup quarterback Mike Kruczek suffered an injury of his own. Suddenly, the Steelers found themselves without any healthy quarterbacks.

Noll looked to Tony, knowing his background as a successful college quarterback. Unexpectedly, Tony's dream of playing quarterback in the NFL was coming true! It was a tough spot, however. Tony hadn't practiced at the position. He didn't know the Steeler offense very well—even the way they did handoffs was different from what Tony had experienced in college. And Tony hadn't worked on his passing for months. Predictably, it didn't go well on the field. Tony fumbled a snap. He and running back Rocky Bleier botched a handoff. And as if that wasn't enough, Tony threw two interceptions while desperately trying to mount a comeback. In doing so, he earned a unique distinction, becoming the only player in NFL history to intercept a pass and throw an interception in the same game.

Tony played just a single quarter as an NFL quarterback. His stats for that game: 3–8, 43 yards, 0 touchdowns, 2 interceptions, 3 rushes for 8 yards.

Pittsburgh lost the game 27–0. Tony was disappointed that he hadn't played better. But the next day, Noll called him into his office. Kruczek was out for the next week. Bradshaw's status was uncertain. Noll told Tony to practice with the quarterbacks that week. There was a small chance he'd have to play the next week!

In the end, Bradshaw was healthy enough to play. But Tony was glad that Noll had enough faith in him to at least consider him for the role.

"I believe I could have [played quarterback in the NFL], given the opportunity," Tony later wrote. "But I didn't get that opportunity. . . . It was time to move on."

The Steelers went 9–5 in the regular season, disappointing by their standards, then lost their opening playoff game to the Denver Broncos, 34–21. In fourteen regular-season games, Tony intercepted three passes, returning them for a total of 37 yards.

Tony worked hard to prepare for the 1978 season. He worked out and added eight pounds of muscle to his body. He also kept studying film and learning the ins and outs of playing safety. As training camp rolled around, he had every reason to feel confident about his place on the team. But a new problem had developed. He was feeling tired and sluggish during his workouts. The team doctor gave him the bad news: he had mononucleosis, or mono. It took him three long weeks to gain his strength back. He missed a big chunk of training camp, putting his chances of making the team in serious jeopardy. But in the end, Noll decided once again to keep Tony.

It was a good decision. Tony was still a backup, starting just two games, but 1978 would be his finest season. The Steelers beat the Buffalo Bills 28–17 in the opener and never looked back. They started the season with seven straight wins. Tony was a big part of the team's defense, which fans called the Steel Curtain. He led the team with 6 interceptions—the second-highest total in the American Football Conference (AFC). One of his biggest interceptions came in week four against the Cleveland Browns. On the last play of the game, as the Browns tried for a game-tying score, Tony picked off a pass and returned it 65 yards. The interception secured a 15–9 Steelers victory.

"It was one of those miracle years," Tony later explained. "It seemed like every time I took the field, the ball was headed my way."

It was a great season for the team as well. The Steelers went 14–2 in the regular season. (The NFL had switched to a sixteen-game schedule.) In the AFC playoffs, they dominated the Broncos and the Oilers. The wins sent them to Miami, Florida, to face the Dallas Cowboys in the Super Bowl.

The Steel Curtain

The Steelers of the late 1970s were known for their punishing, shut-down defense. Fans affectionately referred to the team's defensive line—and later the entire defense—as the Steel Curtain. Players like "Mean" Joe Greene, L. C. Greenwood, and Dwight White struck fear into the hearts of opposing offenses.

Bradshaw was on fire in the Super Bowl. He passed for 318 yards and 4 touchdowns to give the Steelers a big lead. The Cowboys tried to stage a late comeback, but they fell short. The Steelers walked away the victors, 35–31. In just his second NFL season, Tony was a Super Bowl champion!

Twenty-three-year-old Tony was eager to start the 1979 season with the Steelers. "We had a great year in '78 and had just about everybody back," he later said. "So you felt like [Pittsburgh was] going to have a good year again and I was looking forward to being a part of that."

Once again, Tony worked out tirelessly in the off-season and reported to training camp in great shape. And for once, he didn't think his place on the team was in question. He was so confident that he even bought a home in the area. But things didn't work out quite as planned. Noll was struggling to make the team's final cuts. Tony was too strong a player to cut outright. So instead, Noll traded him for a future tenth-round draft pick. Just before the regular season began, Tony got the bad news. He'd been traded from the league's best team to its worst—the San Francisco 49ers.

The Steelers' success continued after Tony left in 1979. They repeated as Super Bowl champs, defeating the Los Angeles Rams 31–19.

Playing in San Francisco was a lot different from Pittsburgh. The 49ers were terrible, finishing at just 2–14 in 1979. Tony played in fifteen games and even started in seven of them. But he failed to reproduce his success of the previous year and didn't intercept a single pass. He also spent some time as the team's punt returner, with little success.

In the off-season, the 49ers traded Tony to the New York Giants. Tony went to training camp with the Giants, but he was among the team's final cuts. It was the end of Tony's career as an NFL player. It was time to move on to the next phase of his life.

Chapter Five

A New Career

Tony wasn't ready to give up on football entirely. He'd been told that his understanding of the game made him a great candidate to be a coach someday. So he headed back to the University of Minnesota. There, he could work out with the Gophers while he volunteered as the team's defensive backs coach under Stoll. It was a great chance for him to try his hand at coaching while cheering on his Gophers. With Tony's help, the team finished the season 5–6, 4–5 in the Big Ten.

Late in the 1980 season, the Denver Broncos called Tony, asking him to join their team as a safety. But Tony had missed so much time that he didn't believe he could be an effective player. He declined the offer.

The experience paid off. After the 1980 season, Giants head coach Ray Perkins called Tony to offer him a coaching position. Tony was ready to accept the offer, but before he did, he got another call. Chuck Noll had heard that the Giants were offering Tony a job. He wanted his former player in Pittsburgh instead. So Tony went back to the Steelers as an assistant coach. At twenty-five years old, he became the youngest coach in the NFL. In fact, many of the players were older than Tony!

❝Basically, everything I do, in terms of coaching and my style and what I want to get done, I borrowed from Coach Noll. I was [with him] as a player and a coach and that's where I learned about professional football and what it takes to win. His philosophy was you do whatever it takes, you get guys who are willing to do whatever it takes and then you become a fundamentally sound team. You pay attention to details. . . . There's a certain way you win in the NFL and that's by execution. So that philosophy I've kept with me ever since then.❞

—TONY ON CHUCK NOLL'S INFLUENCE ON HIS COACHING STYLE

Tony was essentially Noll's right-hand man. One of his most important jobs was to break down game film, helping Noll analyze opponents as well as the Steelers' performance. Coaching was a big change in Tony's professional life, and his personal life was about to go through a big change as well. In the summer of 1981, he was invited to speak at a father-son breakfast at a Pittsburgh church. He made an impression on the church's pastor, Dr. John Guest, who insisted on setting up a date for Tony with a young woman from the church, Lauren Harris.

Tony was reluctant at first. He was very shy around women and had never even had a serious girlfriend. But after weeks of prodding, Guest finally convinced him to meet Lauren. Tony really liked her. She shared his Christian faith and many of his values. Soon the two started dating. They went to church together and played tennis, and Tony taught her about football. A few months later, Tony asked Lauren to marry him. She agreed, and on June 19, 1982, the couple was married. Dr. Guest performed the ceremony.

Tony continued as an assistant coach in 1982 and 1983. In 1984 a new professional football league, the United States Football League (USFL) formed to compete with the NFL. Pittsburgh's defensive coordinator, Woody Widenhofer, left the Steelers for a job as head coach for the Oklahoma Outlaws. Noll needed a new defensive coordinator. Tony knew the team's system and the players, and he believed he'd be the best man for the job. Noll agreed.

"Nobody knows as much about our defense as you do," Noll told him. "That's always been my thought process since Woody left. You're our defensive coordinator."

With the promotion, twenty-eight-year-old Tony became the league's youngest unit coordinator. Many NFL experts thought he would probably replace Noll one day and could possibly be the first African American head coach in the NFL.

Tony had two head-coaching interviews early in his coaching career. He interviewed with the Philadelphia Eagles in 1986 and with the Green Bay Packers in 1987. But according to most reports, he wasn't seriously considered for either job. Some people speculated that he was interviewed only so that the teams could claim they had considered minority candidates.

More big news came the summer before the 1984 season— Lauren gave birth to the couple's first child, Tiara. Tony's life revolved around his daughter, his wife, and his defense. He had more responsibility than ever with the Steelers. He had to form the entire game plan for the Steelers' defense. He had to run the defensive practices and give Noll input on which players to keep and which players to start. In his first season as the defensive

41

coordinator, the Steelers went 9–7 in the regular season. Tony's defense allowed a total of 310 points, eleventh best in the league. Pittsburgh won its opening playoff game against Denver 24–17. But Tony's defense crumbled in the AFC Championship against the Miami Dolphins. Rookie quarterback Dan Marino torched Pittsburgh in a 45–28 loss.

The Steelers' time as an NFL powerhouse was over. The team, including Tony's defense, struggled over the next several years, falling to 7–9 in 1985, 6–10 in 1986, and 8–7 in 1987. (A players' strike during the 1987 season shortened the schedule and forced teams to use replacement players for several games.) The team's poor play reached a new low in 1988. The Steelers went 5–11. Tony's defense allowed 421 points, making it one of the worst defenses in the league.

Noll had to make a change. After the miserable 1988 season, Noll asked Tony to give up his position as defensive coordinator and instead take a position as the team's defensive backs coach. It would have been a huge demotion, and Tony decided that it was time to move on. He resigned from Noll's coaching staff and started to look for a new job in another city. The news was especially tough on Lauren, who had lived in Pittsburgh all her life.

Luckily, coaches around the league had plenty of interest in Tony. Almost right away, he got calls from four teams: the Giants, the 49ers, the Kansas City Chiefs, and the Cincinnati Bengals.

At first, Tony was leaning toward taking a job with the Bengals. He had worked with Coach Sam Wyche while playing for San Francisco in 1979, and Cincinnati was close to Pittsburgh and Lauren's family. But the offer fell through, and Tony had to reconsider. He and Lauren talked and decided that Kansas City was the best fit. He took a job with the Chiefs as the defensive backs coach. It was a step backward in his coaching career. But Tony was ready to work hard and earn another coordinator position.

Life in Kansas City was difficult. The coaching style of Marty Schottenheimer was very different from Noll's. Tony was used to Noll's relaxed, family-oriented style. With the Chiefs, however, he was working all the time. Schottenheimer expected his coaches to live, eat, and breathe football. This was tough for Tony. Lauren had recently given birth to a son, Jamie. Tony wanted to spend more time with his young family, but he made the best of it.

❝I don't think there is a more deliberate and organized coach in the NFL. Marty might spend forty-five minutes [analyzing] one play or one series until it is right.❞

—TONY ON MARTY SCHOTTENHEIMER

The Chiefs made the playoffs in both 1990 and 1991. The defense, including Tony's defensive backfield, was among the best in the league. In 1991, it allowed an average of just 15.8 points per game, seventh best in the NFL.

After the 1991 season, Chuck Noll retired from the Steelers. The Chiefs' defensive coordinator, Bill Cowher, took his place as the new head coach. Cowher's departure opened up the coordinator position in Kansas City. Tony was confident that Schottenheimer would give him the job. After all, the head coach had once told Tony that if Cowher ever left, he was in line for the position. But Schottenheimer didn't live up to his word. Instead, the head coach offered the job to one of his close friends, Dave Adolph.

Tony was angry. He knew it was time to leave Kansas City. In January 1992, the Minnesota Vikings hired Dennis Green as their new head coach. (Green was just the second African American head coach in the NFL. The first was Art Shell.) Green, who had coached the special teams in San Francisco when Tony played there in 1979, asked Tony to be his defensive coordinator. Tony accepted—a decision that didn't please Lauren, who was dreading the cold Minnesota winters. The family, which now included a second son, Eric, packed their things and headed to Minneapolis.

It turned out to be a great decision for Tony. Green took Tony under his wing, teaching him the ins and outs of being a head coach. Tony helped Green handle media relations, which was a responsibility few head coaches give to their assistants.

Green included Tony on most major decisions with the team, even those that didn't affect the defense.

Dennis Green had a tumultuous relationship with the media, and Tony often found himself speaking for the coach. It was just one way Tony's cool, calm style perfectly complemented that of the fiery Green.

Tony's defensive style was a good fit for Minnesota. He orchestrated an aggressive defense that focused on getting take-aways (interceptions and fumbles). He didn't just want his defense to stop the other team from scoring. He also wanted them to get into the end zone, which was a growing trend in the NFL.

"I believe there are three factors for the increase in defensive scoring," Tony told a reporter in 1992. "First, creating turnovers by stripping the ball has become a staple of the league. With more turnovers, there are more opportunities for defensive touchdowns. Next, there is more overall team speed on defense. Even guys on the defensive line and guys in the middle ... when they pick up fumbles, not too many [players] on offense can catch them. And finally, with everybody using [so many receivers], there basically isn't anybody left near the line of scrimmage that can catch a defensive player running the other way."

With Tony's aggressive approach, the Vikings' defense was among the best in the league. In 1993 it was ranked number one in the entire NFL, allowing opposing offenses just 4,406 yards. In 1994 the Vikings' defense scored a league-high seven touchdowns. More important, Tony's great defense helped Minnesota reach the playoffs in three of his four years with the team.

Tony was enjoying a lot of success in Minnesota. Many experts believed that it was only a matter of time before he'd be a head coach.

Chapter Six

Coach Dungy

As the Vikings' defensive coordinator, Tony was young, energetic, successful, well liked by his players, and respected around the league. A few teams had interviewed him for their head-coaching positions, but he had not received an offer. To many, it didn't make sense.

Tony gave two possible reasons for why he didn't yet have a head-coaching job. "People are enthralled with winners, I mean Super Bowl winners. . . . But not every head-coach-to-be won a Super Bowl before he got a head-coaching job, so that shouldn't be the only qualification. And that leads to the second and probably the biggest reason. Owners have a perception of what a head coach is. I don't fit that bill. It's perception. There are only two black head coaches in the league, so that about says it all. Sometimes it's upsetting, but there is nothing I can do about it."

After the 1995 season, only two teams were looking for a new head coach—the Miami Dolphins and the Tampa Bay Buccaneers. Both teams wanted former Dallas Cowboys coach Jimmy Johnson, so Tony knew that left only one opening. He wasn't optimistic about his chances. He figured that his best chance was if Tampa hired Johnson, because he didn't think the Bucs' ownership was very interested in him. So when Johnson agreed to a contract with the Dolphins, it looked like another year (at least) in Minnesota.

Surprisingly, Tony did get a call from the Bucs. Their general manager, Rich McKay, wanted to meet with him. Without getting his hopes up too much, Tony headed to Florida. Then came a second meeting. The media was reporting that Tony had become one of the top candidates for the job.

A SCREW LOOSE

Tony's first interview with the Buccaneers was somewhat of a disaster. On his way to the meeting, he lost one of the screws that held his glasses together. He didn't have a backup pair, so he couldn't see much during the meeting. And even more embarrassing, he tried to wear the broken glasses for about half the meeting, even though they barely stayed on his face.

Then Tony got the call he'd been waiting years to get. McKay and the Bucs were ready to make an offer. At forty years old, Tony was going to be Tampa Bay's next head coach!

Tony was in for a big challenge. Tampa had long been one of the NFL's worst teams. Players, coaches, and fans alike thought of the Bucs as a losing team. Tony had to change that mind-set. His slogan for the team was "No excuses, no explanations." It meant that every person in the Tampa locker room was responsible for his own actions, both on and off the field.

THE HAPLESS BUCS

The Tampa Bay Buccaneers joined the NFL as an expansion team in 1976. The team played its first year in the AFC West division, but it was moved to the NFC Central in 1977 (and then to the new NFC South in 2002). Tampa's early history was filled with losses, including their first 26 games. They briefly enjoyed success, winning the NFC Central in 1979 and 1981, before falling back into NFL obscurity. The team floundered for fifteen years before Tony took over and made them a perennial contender.

His first regular-season game as a head coach came at home against the Green Bay Packers on September 1, 1996.

He believed in his team and expected them to compete against the Packers, one of the NFL's best teams. But after the first half, Tony and the Bucs were behind 24–3. Things didn't get any better in the second half, and the Packers cruised to a 34–3 victory. It was a forgettable debut for Tony and his team.

The losses kept coming. The Detroit Lions easily handled Tampa in the second game, 21–6. Then the Bucs blew a chance for a win against the Denver Broncos. In the fourth game, the Bucs jumped out to a lead against the Seattle Seahawks, but they let Seattle come back for the win. In the fifth game, the Lions dismantled the Bucs 27–0.

At 0–5, things looked bleak. But Tony wasn't ready to give up, even with Green and the powerful Vikings coming to Tampa for the sixth game. "This is a perfect setup to get our first win," he told his players. "We've had a good week of practice and we're the healthiest we've been all season. [The Vikings are] the best team in the NFL, but we're getting better every week. Our plan is solid, but this won't be a 'game-plan game.' It will be a passion game. Execution. Attitude. Protect the ball. Have a little swagger."

The players responded. Their surprising 24–13 home victory over the Vikings gave Tony his first win as a head coach and gave the long-suffering Bucs fans at least a glimmer of hope.

The Bucs went on to lose their next three games to fall to 1–8. Tony had remained calm with his team throughout the season. He didn't like to yell and scream. It wasn't his style. But that changed before the tenth game, against the Oakland Raiders. A couple of Tony's players had neglected to show up for off-the-field engagements, including a visit to a local classroom. Tony was furious. When he finally did lay into his team, it had nothing to do with football. He wanted players who kept their word, and he left no confusion: anyone who didn't want to follow through on his promises was welcome to find a new team. Tony wanted players who had integrity as well as talent. He later admitted that it was his biggest locker-room blowup in his coaching career.

❝Coach challenged us to be more than just a winning football team. He wanted us to be winners in life—and he led by example.❞

—TAMPA BAY LINEBACKER DERRICK BROOKS

Whether by coincidence or because of Tony's emotional speech, the Bucs' season seemed to turn around from that point. They beat the Raiders 20–17 later that week. The next week, they ended a ten-game road losing streak by beating the San Diego Chargers 25–17 (despite falling behind 14–0 to start the game). They improved their record to 5–10 entering the season's final game. Tony told his players to treat the final game against the

Chicago Bears as a playoff game. They listened, and as a result they dominated Chicago from start to finish. As the final seconds of the game, and the season, ticked away, the Tampa players doused Tony with Gatorade. It was an unusual way for a team to celebrate what was, in the standings, a meaningless win. But Tony and the Bucs understood that it was far from meaningless. The franchise was trying to shed its "loser" label, and the win over Chicago was a big part of doing exactly that.

After the 1–8 start, the Bucs had gone 5–2 in their final seven games. They had a punishing defense, highlighted by Tony's famous cover-2 defense (commonly called the Tampa 2 or the Minnesota Cover 2), which prevented deep passes and focused on creating turnovers. They selected an electrifying running back, Warrick Dunn, in the 1997 draft. Everything was coming together for Tony's second season. For the first time in years, Bucs fans were optimistic.

The opening game, at home against San Francisco, would be a big test. The 49ers, led by quarterback Steve Young, were one of the league's best teams. But the Bucs were up to the challenge. Defensive tackle Warren Sapp burst through the 49ers' offensive line on the game's fifth play and slammed into Young, knocking him out of the game with a concussion (bruise to the brain). Later, Sapp tackled receiver Jerry Rice and knocked him out of the game as well.

At halftime, San Francisco led 6–0. The Bucs looked poised to take the lead, but they fumbled the ball at the 49ers' 4-yard line. It was the sort of play that would have caused many Bucs teams of the past to give up. But Tony wouldn't allow that. Two field goals and a Trent Dilfer touchdown pass gave Tampa a 13–6 lead, and Sapp and the defense made it hold up. "I could feel the confidence permeating our locker room," Tony later wrote.

The team had every reason to be confident. With Dunn darting out of the backfield and the defense dominating opposing offenses, the Bucs beat the Lions 24–17. They moved to 3–0 for the season with a convincing 28–14 win over the Vikings in Minnesota. Tony's team was elated, but he reminded them to be restrained. He told his players to act like they'd expected to win and not like they were surprised by it. It was just another part of building a culture of winning in the Tampa locker room.

The winning streak continued in week four. The Bucs hosted the Miami Dolphins, an in-state rival led by the legendary Dan Marino. The Tampa crowd was rocking as Tony's team cruised to a 31–21 victory, highlighted by a 58-yard pass reception by Dunn. The team pushed its record to 5–0 the next week with a 19–18 win over the Arizona Cardinals, although that win was secured only when Arizona's kicker missed a 47-yard field goal attempt.

The Bucs cooled off late in the season, including two losses to Green Bay that prevented them from winning the National Football Conference (NFC) Central division title. But with a 10–6 record, they had earned a trip to the playoffs as a Wild Card (one of the top teams not to win its division). It was Tampa's first trip to the playoffs in fifteen years. The team's late-season struggles were all but forgotten as they prepared to host the Lions in the first round of the playoffs.

STAYING HOME

The Buccaneers had already clinched a playoff spot entering the final game of the 1997 season against Chicago. But the game was still important. With a loss, they'd have to play on the road. A win would earn them a home game. The team, knowing how important home-field advantage was, won the game 35–17.

The Tampa players and fans were excited. "I've never been [to the playoffs]," said linebacker Derrick Brooks. "Sunday's a long way away. . . . I'm pretty pumped. We're hungry. We've made the cake. Now we've got to put the icing on it [with a win]."

Previously, Detroit's star running back, Barry Sanders, had run all over the Tampa defense in one of the teams' regular-season matchups. Sapp and the defense were determined not to let that happen again. They held the dangerous Sanders to 65 rushing yards, while Dunn, Dilfer, and the rest of the offense did enough to secure a 20–10 victory. As the final whistle sounded, some of the Bucs players stormed the field with team flags, while others went up into the stands to celebrate with the fans. The game was the final one played in Tampa Stadium. The Buccaneers would be playing in the new Raymond James Stadium beginning in 1998.

After the game, Dilfer gave all the credit for the win to Tony. "[Tony] got us ready and made up for the playoff inexperience," he said. "Coach Dungy got us ready by emphasizing the energy level. By telling us the importance of limiting mistakes. And by telling us to have fun. And when we are as physical as we were today, that takes care of a lot of things."

❝We've come a long way from 0–5 in 1996. I felt like we came out confident and beat a really good football team in a really big game. We handled ourselves well. Now we've got to get better on some little detail things and get ready to play a very good Green Bay team.❞
—TONY ON HIS FIRST PLAYOFF VICTORY AS A HEAD COACH

Tampa's reward for the playoff victory was a trip to Green Bay to play the defending Super Bowl champs. Despite frigid conditions (including a windchill of 11 degrees Fahrenheit) that heavily favored the cold-weather Packers, the Tampa defense played well, forcing Packers quarterback Brett Favre into two big interceptions. But the offense couldn't capitalize. The Packers overcame their mistakes and showed why they were the champs in a 21–7 victory that ended a remarkable turnaround season for Tony and the Bucs. After the game, Tony felt a mix of disappointment and pride. The season hadn't ended the way he had hoped, but his team had finally shed the loser label that had followed it for so many years. The future looked bright.

Chapter Seven

Highs and Lows in Tampa

The Buccaneers and their fans had every reason to be optimistic entering the 1998 season. Most experts predicted that they would battle for the NFC Central title with powerhouses Minnesota and Green Bay. The Bucs had a brand-new stadium in Tampa, and most of their key players from the 1997 season were returning.

After losing the first two games on the road in Minnesota and Green Bay, Tampa hosted the Bears in their home opener. The crowd was loud and eager to celebrate a Bucs victory. But the team came out flat and quickly fell behind 15–0. In the second half, however, the Bucs stormed back to earn a thrilling 27–15 comeback victory. Tony was pleased with the victory, but he knew his team hadn't played up to its ability.

"We only played thirty minutes of football today," he told reporters. "We've got to play sixty minutes next week."

The inconsistent play in the win over the bears summed up the whole season for Tampa. They'd look great in one game and terrible in the next.

One example of how good they could be came in week nine against the undefeated Vikings. The Bucs used their stout defense to contain the Viking offense, which would go on to set an NFL record for points. Fullback Mike Alstott ran for 128 yards and scored the winning touchdown in a 27–24 Tampa victory. It was the only regular-season loss the 15–1 Vikings would suffer all year.

But for every flash of brilliance, there was a letdown. The Bucs lost twice to a poor New Orleans Saints team and gave up a late lead in a loss to the Jacksonville Jaguars. Despite the medio-cre play, the 7–8 Bucs headed into the final game of the season with a shot at a return to the playoffs. They needed to beat the Bengals in Cincinnati and then hope the San Diego Chargers, who had gone 5–10, could beat the Cardinals in a late game.

The Bucs handled their end of the deal, completely domi-nating the Bengals in a 35–0 blowout. But as the team flew home, the pilot gave them the bad news. The Cardinals had kicked a game-winning field goal on the final play to secure the last NFC playoff spot. After the excitement of the 1997 season, Tony's Bucs had taken a big step backward, finishing 8–8 and out of the playoffs.

Tony was the starting quarterback for his high school football team in Jackson, Michigan, for three years.

Tony played defensive back for the Pittsburgh Steelers for the 1977 season and the Super Bowl-winning 1978 season.

Tony stands on the field before a game at Three Rivers Stadium in 1981. Tony was the Steelers' defensive backs coach from 1981 to 1983.

Tony stands on the sidelines during the Buccaneers' NFC Division Championship game in 2000.

Tony meets with a group of students in Swaziland during a trip to southern Africa with other NFL players and coaches supporting education for the underprivileged.

Tony talks to Colts quarterback Peyton Manning.

Tony speaks to the media after the funeral for his son Jamie in 2006.

Tony and his son Eric acknowledge the crowd before a Colts game in 2006. This was Tony's first game back after Jamie's death.

Tony and his wife, Lauren, celebrate the Colts' AFC Championship in 2007.

Tony sits on the shoulders of his assistant coaches after beating the Chicago Bears to win the Super Bowl in 2007.

To Tony the 1998 team was better than the 1997 team, at least in terms of talent. But the 1998 team hadn't taken advantage of its opportunities, and it had failed to live up to its abilities. He hoped to correct that problem in 1999.

Throughout Tony's career with the Bucs, the team had been known for having a great defense and a sputtering offense. That was never more true than in the beginning of the 1999 season. In the opener, the defense held the Giants to a paltry 107 yards of total offense. But the offense gave up two turnovers that resulted in New York touchdowns, and somehow Tampa lost the game.

In another game early on, the defense led the way in a 6–3 win over the Bears. Dilfer was struggling badly at quarterback, prompting Tony to try backup Eric Zeier for a few games. Zeier didn't fare any better, however, and soon Dilfer was back in. He led the team to three straight wins. Then, in week 12, Dilfer's regular season came to an end when he broke his collarbone in a game against the Seahawks.

Rookie quarterback Shaun King took over and led the team to a 16–3 win over Seattle. King rallied the team to two more wins to extend the winning streak to six games. At 9–4, the Bucs were back among the NFC's best teams. The offense was still lagging far behind the defense, but they were finally doing at least enough to win.

The wins kept coming. Tampa finished with an 11–5 record, a division title, and a first-round bye (week off) in the playoffs—not bad, considering they'd started the season 3–4!

The Bucs finished the 1999 season winning 8 of their last 9 games. But the one loss was troubling—a 45–0 pounding at the hands of the Oakland Raiders.

Tony and his Bucs opened the playoffs at home against the Washington Redskins. The Bucs came out flat, allowing Washington to run up a 13–0 lead. In the third quarter, safety John Lynch intercepted a pass from Redskins quarterback Brad Johnson, and the offense cashed in with a touchdown. Then Sapp crashed into Johnson to force a fumble, and the Bucs scored again. Suddenly, it was 14–13. The Redskins had a chance to win it late, but they botched a 52-yard field goal attempt to give Tampa the victory.

"We won ugly, but so what?" said defensive lineman Steve White. "We shouldn't have to defend the way we play, because it works. People can say our offense is from the Stone Age or whatever. But the fact is there are a lot of teams . . . at home while our style of play has gotten us one win away from the Super Bowl."

It was a thrilling victory for the Bucs and their fans. Even the cool and collected Tony later admitted that it was the most exciting moment of his career. The win earned Tampa a trip to St. Louis to face the Rams. The Rams were the exact opposite of the Bucs. They had a below-average defense but an outstanding offense nicknamed the "Greatest Show on Turf."

The contrast between the two teams made for a lot of pregame excitement. It was the unstoppable force of the Rams offense against the immovable object of the Bucs defense. Which style would prevail? Most experts thought that a high-scoring game would favor St. Louis, while a low-scoring affair would favor Tampa.

It didn't quite work out the way the experts thought. Defense trumped offense on that day. In the first half, each offense managed just a field goal. The Rams added two more points when a snap sailed over King's head and into the end zone for a safety. It was 5–3 St. Louis at halftime, exactly the type of low-scoring contest that many people had assumed Tony and his Bucs would want.

Tampa kicked a field goal in the fourth quarter to take a 1-point lead. The Rams came right back, though. The Tampa defense had been smothering MVP quarterback Kurt Warner all day, but he came through late. The Rams were in field-goal range on a third-and-4 play (third down and four yards to go for a first down). Tony and his coaches tried a blitz (sending extra defenders to rush the quarterback) in hopes of a sack that would knock St. Louis out of field-goal range. But Warner read the defense and made a quick throw downfield to receiver Ricky Proehl. Proehl hauled it in and darted into the end zone for the go-ahead score. Suddenly, Tampa was behind 11–6 with only about four minutes left in the game.

Tony explained why they'd called for the risky blitz: "We wanted to either get them out of field-goal range or make it a longer kick. It's a bitter pill to swallow because we did so much of what we wanted to do. But in the end, they found a way into the end zone."

Despite the disappointment of letting the Rams score, the Bucs weren't finished. They needed a touchdown to punch their tickets to the Super Bowl. The Bucs got the ball back, and King and the offense moved down to the St. Louis 35-yard line. The young quarterback threw a 12-yard pass that receiver Bert Emanuel appeared to catch as he was falling to the turf. The catch would give the Bucs a first down at the 23-yard line with 40 seconds to play. Tony called a time-out to stop the clock.

During the break, the officials decided to review the catch on instant replay. They came back with a decision that shocked almost everyone watching the game—Emanuel hadn't controlled the ball well enough as he fell. One camera angle showed the nose of the football touching the turf, and officials decided that it should be an incompletion (it was a call that later led to changes in the rules for what constitutes a catch in the NFL). King and the offense never recovered, and the Rams held on for the win.

Emanuel and the Bucs felt cheated, but the game—and their season—was over. The Rams went on to win the Super Bowl. The Bucs could only look ahead to 2000 and hope for better things.

Tony was pleased with the way his team had bounced back after the disastrous 1998 season. But Tampa's owners weren't. They were tired of seeing the Bucs' offense fail. So they forced Tony to make some changes to his coaching staff. They insisted that Tony fire offensive coordinator Mike Shula. Tony fought the decision. According to his contract, he had control over the hiring and firing of coaches. Did he dare defy his bosses? He didn't want to fire a friend and someone he believed was doing a good job.

"Everybody thinks that making a coaching change is the way to go," he said. "Most times, it has been my experience that you're just making other difficulties. I think [firing Shula] is wrong." In the end, Shula made it easy on Tony by resigning from the job. Tony hired Les Steckel as his replacement. But the situation was the first sign of trouble with Tony's coaching regime in Tampa.

Expectations were high for the 2000 season. The Bucs' incredible defense was still intact, and King was returning as quarterback with some experience under his belt. The team had traded for star receiver Keyshawn Johnson—a big upgrade for the offense. Fans felt confident that they had a championship-caliber team with a championship-caliber head coach.

A GROWING FAMILY

In August 2000, Tony and Lauren added to their family by adopting another son, Jordan. They soon discovered that their new son had serious medical problems, however. Jordan wasn't able to feel pain. That meant he was often unaware that he was in danger. Pain is an important response that helps people avoid getting hurt. Jordan needed extra care and teaching so he'd know how to keep himself safe. In 2001, the Dungys adopted another child, a daughter named Jade.

Everything started according to plan. The Bucs won the first three games, including a 41–0 blowout against the Bears. The Bucs were looking so good that *Sports Illustrated* suggested they might be able to match Miami's undefeated season in 1972. But any such aspirations quickly went down the drain, starting in week four. Tampa followed the 3–0 start with four straight losses, the last an embarrassing 28–14 defeat to Detroit at home. The Bucs recovered quickly, however, winning seven of their final nine games to finish the season 10–6 and earn a Wild Card playoff berth. A loss to Green Bay in the final regular-season game cost them the division title, however. Minnesota claimed the NFC Central instead.

A Measure of Revenge

Late in the 2000 season, the 9–5 Bucs faced the Rams, the team that had knocked them out of the playoffs the year before, in a Monday night game that they needed to win to secure a playoff berth. Unlike the defensive battle of the previous season, this one was an offensive shootout. Tony and the Bucs needed an unusual play to win the game. Trailing by four, King threw a screen pass (a short pass behind blockers) to Dunn. Dunn was penned in by the St. Louis defense, however, and flipped the ball back to King. King caught it and dashed for a huge 30-yard gain that led to the winning score.

The Bucs traveled to Philadelphia to face the Eagles in the first round of the playoffs. Fans wondered which Tampa team would show up—the one that had inspired talk of an unbeaten season or the one that had gone just 7–6 in its final 13 games. Unfortunately for Tony, his team didn't put its best foot forward when it counted the most. On a bitterly cold day, the Eagles jumped all over the Bucs. Once again, the Tampa offense was inept and the defense just couldn't do enough in a 21–3 loss.

For the second straight year, Tony had to make a change to his coaching staff. After just one season, Steckel was fired. Tony promoted quarterback coach Clyde Christensen to take his place. And rumors were starting to swirl that Tony's own job security might be in jeopardy. He knew that his team would need a great season in 2001.

Unfortunately, the Bucs didn't respond. Once again, they stumbled to a mediocre regular season (9–7) and barely made the playoffs. Even the addition of veteran quarterback Brad Johnson didn't cure the woes of the struggling offense. The season offered some highlights, including another thrilling Monday night victory over the Rams. But Tony knew that success would ultimately be judged by what happened in the playoffs, and in the first round the Bucs faced a familiar foe, the Eagles.

It was a dark time for Tony. Not only was his job on the line, but a week earlier, he had received devastating news. His mother had died after a long battle with diabetes.

The Eagles once again dominated the Bucs. Just as in the previous year's game against Philly, the Tampa offense failed to score a touchdown, and the Buccaneers lost 31–9.

Two days later, Tony got the news that the Bucs had fired him. Tony had helped turn the team from a laughingstock into a perennial contender. But after six years, his time in Tampa had come to an end.

66*As a boss, you have to make decisions. I've made them and done what I think is best for the team. My boss has made his decision on what he thinks is best for the team.*99
—TONY ON GETTING FIRED AS TAMPA'S HEAD COACH

Chapter Eight

A New Start

As Tony was clearing out his office one late-January night, a local news camera crew caught him loading boxes into his vehicle. The video got play on local and national networks. It wasn't the way Tony wanted his end in Tampa to be remembered. But he also realized that it was the reality of the situation. His departure was big news in Tampa and across the NFL. Fortunately, not all the news was bad. The Bucs didn't want him anymore, but several other teams did.

One phone call came from Jim Irsay, the owner of the Indianapolis Colts. The Colts had just fired their head coach, Jim Mora. They were an organization built around a stellar offense, led by star quarterback Peyton Manning. Their defense, however, was consistently among the league's worst. With Tony's defensive track record in Minnesota and Tampa, it seemed like a perfect match. "You're the only person I want for this job," Irsay told him.

In the end, Tony had to choose between the Colts job and a position with the Carolina Panthers. Largely because of Irsay's sincerity, Tony chose to head to Indianapolis. He signed a five-year, $13-million contract just eight days after being fired by the Buccaneers.

One of Tony's first moves as head coach was to sign his longtime friend and former coach Tom Moore as the Colts' new offensive coordinator. Contrary to popular opinion, Tony intended to be just as involved with the Indianapolis offense as with its struggling defense. "I never bought into the idea that Tony was only here to help out our defense," Manning later said. "Tony is the head coach and he's in charge of the whole team."

> ❝I really like [Tony]. I think we're kind of in similar situations, both used to success and having last year not going the way we wanted. I really don't like to get into comparisons with [him] and Coach Mora, but I've gotten to know Tony and he's a pretty player-friendly coach. At the same time, we're still getting the same quality of work done. It's just a good setup.❞
> —PEYTON MANNING ON HIS NEW HEAD COACH

This time Tony wasn't charged with rebuilding a losing team, as he had been in Tampa. While the Colts had posted a disappointing 6–10 record in 2001, many NFL experts saw them as a team on the rise, largely due to the emergence of Manning as one of the league's best quarterbacks. Tony would be expected to have at least some degree of immediate success. Anything short of a playoff berth in 2002 would be a disappointment.

Tony quickly introduced the team to his way of running things. He stressed turnovers—both getting them on defense and avoiding them on offense. He wanted his players to avoid penalties and not to give up big plays. Surprisingly, not all of the big changes he made were to the defense. He also thought there was room for improvement in the offense. Tony felt that he needed to rein in his talented young quarterback. In previous years, Manning had often gotten himself into trouble with interceptions. He was always looking to complete the deep ball. Tony helped Manning learn to look for the short, safe pass more often. Those plays didn't take away from the potency of the Indy offense, but rather added another challenge for opposing defenses.

"Part of me still wants to defend the four years before [Tony] got here," Manning later said. "I was dying at times making those aggressive throws, but that's how we were living too."

Tony had needed six games to get his first win in Tampa. In Indy, he managed it in his first regular-season game of

2002—but it wasn't easy. The Colts traveled to Jacksonville, Florida, for the opener. Their defense was clinging to a 28–25 lead, and Jacksonville had time for just one last play from midfield. Jaguar quarterback Mark Brunell heaved a long pass into the end zone, but it dropped, incomplete—game over. It was a great way to start Tony's career as a Colt.

Indianapolis opened the season 4–1 but then lost three games in a row to even their record at 4–4. That set up a trip to Philadelphia to face the Eagles—the team that had knocked Tony's Bucs out of the playoffs the previous two seasons. The Eagles were a powerful team built on a great defense. In fact, Tony's offenses hadn't mustered a single touchdown against the Eagles in those two playoff games. So when Manning led the Colts' offense to five touchdowns and an easy 35–13 win, Tony had good reason to smile.

The big win turned the season around for the Colts. They went on to finish the regular season at 10–6, good enough for a Wild Card spot in the AFC playoffs.

In the first round, the Colts would face the New York Jets, coached by Herm Edwards, one of Tony's closest friends. On paper, it looked like an even matchup. Tony and his team were brimming with confidence as they took the field.

That confidence was quickly shattered. The Jets rolled over a Colts defense that couldn't seem to do anything right, scoring touchdown after touchdown. Even worse, Manning and the offense played just as poorly. By the time the final whistle sounded, the Jets had a shocking 41–0 victory. It was the fourth straight playoff loss for Tony, and his offenses had failed to score a single touchdown in any of those four losses.

After the embarrassment in New York, Tony watched former Oakland coach Jon Gruden lead the Buccaneers to an NFC title and a trip to the Super Bowl. The Bucs team that Tony had built then beat the Oakland Raiders 48–21 for a Super Bowl championship. It was bittersweet for Tony. After all, he had many great friends back in Tampa and was happy to see them win. But on the other hand, he had to endure watching another coach do what he'd been unable to do.

"I was excited for the team," Tony later wrote. "But it still hurt, not being there with them."

In the off-season, Tony also had to deal with the backlash from the playoff blowout. Critics said that he couldn't win in the playoffs. They said the same of Manning, who was 0–3 in the playoffs in his career. Worse still, not all of the criticism came from outside the organization. Star kicker Mike Vanderjagt made some very critical comments about the team, Manning, and Tony in particular. The kicker said that Tony was too mild-mannered to be a successful coach in the playoffs. Tony considered cutting the talented kicker—a move that most of the other coaches in the league would have made without hesitation. But ultimately Tony decided to give Vanderjagt a second chance, in part at the insistence of his son Jamie.

Tony's patience paid off. Vanderjagt would go on to have an excellent 2003 season. He and his teammates burst out of the gate with four straight wins to open the season, highlighted by a 55–21 win over the New Orleans Saints in which Manning threw six touchdown passes.

TONY'S ULTIMATUM

Before a game in Jacksonville in 2003, a security guard told Tony that his eleven-year-old son, Eric, wasn't allowed on the field with him. The guard insisted that Eric leave. Tony wouldn't hear of it. His sons had spent countless hours by his side during his coaching career. He told the guard that if Eric was removed, the Colts would leave the field and force the game to be postponed. The guard left, and Tony never heard another word about having his family members on the field.

The hot start set up one of the most anticipated matchups of the season. The Colts traveled to Tampa Bay to face the defending champions on *Monday Night Football*. It was Tony's first time facing his old team, and it was on national television. And, as if that wasn't enough, it was Tony's forty-eighth birthday.

"Pregame was such a special experience," Tony later wrote. "I visited with the Buccaneers coaches, players, and staff on the field. I was experiencing so many emotions and so many good memories, I'm afraid I wasn't much use to the Colts during pregame, as I spent most of my time trying not to cry."

Tony was nervous about the reception he would get from the Tampa fans. Would they boo him? He was relieved and touched, however, when he got a rousing standing ovation during introductions. At that moment, Tony couldn't hold back the tears.

Despite the emotion, Tony had an important game to coach. Indianapolis's chances at moving to 5–0 looked pretty dim in the fourth quarter. Tampa had been in control while building a 14-point lead. Manning and the offense had the ball, hoping to drive for a touchdown that would cut the lead to 7. But early in the drive, Manning dropped back and threw a pass over the middle that safety Ronde Barber intercepted and ran back for a touchdown. With the score at 35–14, viewers across the nation flicked their TVs off. Only about four minutes remained, and the Bucs appeared to have put the finishing touches on a big win.

No team in NFL history had ever come back to win a game from 21 points down with so little time remaining. But Tony and the Colts weren't ready to give up. After marching down the field in record time, running back James Mungro ran for a 3-yard score to trim the lead to 14. Tony had his team try an onside kick (a short kick that either team can recover). The gamble worked, and the Colts got the ball back. Manning led the offense on another frantic drive. The Colts needed just over a minute to score again, as Manning connected with star receiver Marvin Harrison for a 28-yard touchdown.

The Tampa offense couldn't do anything with the ensuing possession. The Colts forced a punt, and with 1:14 on the clock, the offense took the field once again. Manning wasted no time, hitting Troy Walters with a short pass before connecting with Harrison on a 52-yard pass that brought the Colts to Tampa's 5-yard line. On the next play, running back Ricky Williams punched it into the end zone, completing the comeback. The Colts had scored three touchdowns in less than four minutes to tie the game!

The game went to overtime, and Vanderjagt once again came through by kicking the game-winning field goal. Somehow—and just barely—the Colts had managed a 38–35 win and moved to 5–0.

Tony had mixed emotions after the game. "I'm just extremely happy," he said. "But when you fight against guys that you've gone to war with . . . It was really tough out there."

The Colts finally lost a game the following week, 23–20 in overtime to Carolina. But they went on to a 12–4 record for 2003 and an AFC South division title. It was a great regular season, but Tony, Manning, and the rest of the Colts knew that it wouldn't mean anything if they didn't finally find some playoff success. They would get their chance against the Denver Broncos in the opening round. The pressure was especially intense for Manning. Critics still said he couldn't win a big game.

The game against the Broncos was another playoff blow-out. But this time, it was in Indianapolis's favor. The Colts scored on their opening drive and never looked back. Manning was nearly flawless as he led the offense up and down the field. The defense did its part as well, and by the final whistle, the Colts had an impressive 41–10 victory.

"I hope people think this was a big game," Tony told the press afterward. "We kept hearing about Peyton's failure to win big games. I guess this was a big one."

❝[Tony is] calm on opening kickoff, and he's calm when you're down 21–3. . . . He's just a cool customer. I think that really spreads through the rest of the team, that it cannot be a panic situation and you can't try to get it all back at once.❞

—PEYTON MANNING ON TONY'S DEMEANOR

The Colts then traveled to Kansas City to face the Chiefs, a team that was in many ways a mirror image of Indianapolis. Both teams relied on powerful offenses and struggled to make up for subpar defenses. As expected, the game was an offensive shootout. Both defenses were so inept that for the first time in playoff history, neither team punted during the game. In the end, Tony and Manning led the Colts to a 38–31 victory and a trip to the AFC title game, giving the Chiefs their only home loss of the season. They were just a win away from a trip to the Super Bowl!

A large roadblock stood in their way, however, in the New England Patriots. The Patriots were the most complete team in the league, with a stellar offense led by quarterback Tom Brady and a powerful defense to match. That defense dominated Peyton and the offense throughout the game, and the Patriots ended Indy's Super Bowl dreams with a 24–14 victory.

"[The Patriots] did a good job defending us, but we did things we haven't done," Tony explained. "We made some miscues, and New England is a good enough team to take advantage of that."

In the summer of 2004, Tony's father died of leukemia. The loss of his father caused him to think about his relationship with his own kids. For the first time in his career, he seriously considered retirement from coaching to spend more time with his family. But in the end, he decided that he hadn't yet finished his job in Indy.

Fishing is one of Tony's favorite pastimes. He also likes to ride his bike, go hiking, and attend sporting events.

With good reason, Tony entered the 2004 season full of optimism. He had the game's best quarterback in Manning, and the defense was slowly improving. After opening with a loss to New England, the Colts caught fire, winning 12 of their next 14 games. They lost a meaningless final game to finish at 12–4. Manning was throwing touchdowns at a historic pace, and while the defense still had its share of tough days, it was clearly improving. Manning broke Dan Marino's single-season touchdown record in late December in a come-from-behind overtime win against the San Diego Chargers, and the Colts locked up another AFC South title and a home game in the first round of the playoffs.

Once again, the Colts hosted Denver in the playoffs. And once again, the Colts easily handled the Broncos, 49–24. The Denver defense could do nothing to stop Manning and his receivers, Harrison, Reggie Wayne, and Brandon Stokley. Denver safety John Lynch—a former player of Tony's in Tampa Bay—admitted after the game that the Colts had the best offense he'd ever seen.

The next round brought a trip to New England's Gillette Stadium to play the Patriots, a familiar nemesis for Tony and the Colts. The Colts were good enough to play with any team in the NFL, but the Patriots, with Tom Brady and head coach Bill Belichick, just seemed to have Indy's number. That didn't change this time around. New England dominated the Colts on both sides of the ball and cruised to a 20–3 victory. Many football experts commented that Tony's team wasn't physical enough to compete with New England. The Patriots' defenders manhandled Indy's receivers all day long and harried Manning in the pocket.

Tony wasn't about to make excuses. "We just ran into a better team today," he said. Nobody could argue. The Colts were one of the NFL's best teams. But they weren't yet ready to compete with the powerful Patriots.

Chapter Nine

To the Top

Throughout the string of playoff disappointments, Tony tried to keep himself and the team on an even keel. He believed that the Colts had what it took to be a championship team. They just had to execute. Tony told his team that doing the little things right is what separates champions from also-rans. He wanted a team that was fundamentally sound and as mistake free as possible.

Early in 2005, the Colts fit that description perfectly. The team came out of the gates hot, both on offense and defense. They dominated the Baltimore Ravens 24–7 in the opener and just kept going from there. A new star was emerging in defensive end Dwight Freeney, and at long last the Colts seemed to be evolving into a complete team.

Indy was 5–0 when they faced the Rams on *Monday Night Football*. The Rams jumped out to an early 17–0 lead, but Tony's calm presence on the sidelines prevented the team from panicking. The team was patient and methodical as it came back for a 45–28 victory, moving their record to 6–0. Around this time, fans and media began wondering whether the Colts could become the NFL's first undefeated team since the 1972 Dolphins.

That question would be asked again and again as the Colts continued to win. And the Colts weren't just winning. They were destroying their competition. In the eighth game, they faced New England. This would be the true test, according to many experts. Would Indy finally get over the hump and beat the Patriots? The answer couldn't have been much clearer—Tony's Colts continued their domination with a 40–21 win over the defending Super Bowl champs.

Tony knew the media would make a big deal over the win but didn't want his players to become overly confident. "We won big today, but let's not forget how we did it," he told them. "We worked hard. This was only one game, and now it's over. We need to continue to do what we do."

The Colts did exactly that. Their winning streak kept growing, as did the pressure. An undefeated season was starting to look like a real possibility. A 45–37 win over the Cincinnati Bengals pushed Indy's record to 10–0. With wins over the Steelers, Titans, and Jaguars, it grew to 13–0. The Colts had just three games left in the season. Could they win all three?

The team had already clinched the AFC South as well as a first-round bye in the playoffs. Those were good things, but they also added another element of pressure for Tony. Often, a team that has wrapped up what it needs to accomplish in the regular season will rest its players for a game or two before the playoffs. It's a chance to get healthy and rested and to be in peak physical shape for the postseason.

But with a historic season on the line, could Tony afford to sit his players? If they lost a game because he let Manning have a week off, he'd be heavily criticized. But on the other hand, if Manning or another key player suffered an injury during an essentially meaningless game, the criticism would be even louder.

"Those guys want to play, and they want to play all the time," Tony told reporters when asked what he'd do. "We don't let them vote, but we will take into consideration how they feel."

On December 22, the importance of an undefeated regular season was put into perspective for Tony and everyone in the Colts organization. Early that morning, Tony got a phone call that no parent ever wants to get. His son Jamie had taken his own life. The reasons for the bright, friendly young man's suicide were never really clear. Tony and Lauren relied heavily on their religious faith to get through the painful ordeal. Tony took some time away from the team to be with his family.

❝_Parents, hug your kids every chance you get. Tell them that you love them every chance you get. You don't know when it's going to be the last time._**❞**

—TONY AT JAMIE'S FUNERAL

"I think God gives you tests to see if you're going to stay true to what you believe and stay faithful," Tony later said. "And for me that's what it was. I think it was really a test."

The Colts didn't get their undefeated season. They lost two of their final three games to finish at 14–2. Tony returned to his team before the last game of the season. The Colts had told him to take the rest of the regular season off, but Tony needed football. He needed to get back into his routine. For him, that was a part of the healing process.

The Colts didn't finish the season with a happy ending, however. After a first-round bye, they hosted the Steelers. Pittsburgh had struggled early in the season but had gotten hot at the end and rode that hot streak to a 21–18 victory (and eventually to a Super Bowl title). Once again, Indy's season was over far earlier than Tony, his team, or their fans would have liked. Their great season already seemed like a distant memory.

Once again, Tony seriously considered retirement after the 2005 season. And once again, he decided to return and try to finish the job he'd started in Indy. Many experts said the Colts' "window of opportunity" was closing. The team was getting older. Star running back Edgerrin James had left the team via free agency. If Indy was going to win a Super Bowl, they had to hurry up and do it.

Tony started writing his autobiography, *Quiet Strength*, in late 2005. The book was published in 2007 and reached the number one spot on the *New York Times* best-seller list.

In their trademark fashion, the Colts started the season red-hot. They won their opener over the Giants (quarterbacked by Peyton Manning's younger brother Eli) and just kept winning. A come-from-behind win over the Tennessee Titans pushed their record to 5–0. The Colts were 9–0 after a 17–16 victory over the Buffalo Bills. But all was not well. The defense had taken a step backward. Opposing teams had learned that they could have great success running the ball against the Colts. A methodical running attack had the added bonus of keeping Manning and the offense off the field. The Cowboys beat them, ending their winning streak at nine games. Then the low point of the season came on December 10 against Jacksonville. The Jaguars' running game gashed the Indy defense time and again, racking up 375 rushing yards in the game—the second-highest single-game rushing total in the NFL since 1970. The 44–17 loss was an embarrassment and a serious cause for concern for Colts fans. After the 9–0 start, the Colts stumbled to a 3–4 finish.

"That thud you just heard was the bottom dropping out on the Colts defense, specifically their futile efforts to stop teams from running the ball right down their throat," wrote national NFL columnist Don Banks. In the newspapers, on TV, and on sports radio shows around the country, the sentiment was much the same.

LENDING A HAND

Tony is involved with many charity organizations. He's a spokesman for the American Diabetes Association and helps to raise money for the Carson Scholars Fund, which provides scholarship money to students from the Indianapolis area. He donates tickets for every Colts home game to the Big Brothers Big Sisters mentoring organization. He also helped to set up the All-Pro Dad program. Through this program, Tony helps dads stay active and involved in their children's lives.

While Colts fans panicked, Tony remained calm. In his classic style, he didn't focus on what he couldn't change, but instead on what he could. "The thing I told the team is that we will see what we are made of from here," he said. "It's fixable. We are going to have to get it fixed to get where we want to go."

The late-season collapse cost the Colts a first-round bye. After such a promising start, the team seemed to be set up for another playoff disappointment. With their terrible run defense, few experts thought they would do serious damage in the playoffs.

Tony had an ace up his sleeve, however. Star safety Bob Sanders had missed most of the regular season because of an injury, but he was back for the playoffs—and just in time. The Colts' opponent was Kansas City, a team led by one of the strongest running games in the NFL. On paper, the Chiefs seemed perfectly suited to give the Colts an early exit, but Sanders and the defense did what few experts expected and shut down the Kansas City running attack. Manning did his part as well, and the Colts advanced with a 23–8 win.

Next, Tony took his team to Baltimore to face the Ravens. And again, the defense stepped up—in fact, they carried the team. Neither team scored a touchdown, but Indy and their new kicker, Adam Vinatieri, won a battle of field goals 15–6 to give Tony his third trip to a championship game as a head coach. He was 0–2 in his previous trips.

Once again, the New England Patriots stood between the Colts and the Super Bowl. But this time, the game would be held in Indianapolis. Tony hoped that home-field advantage would help his team finally get past Brady and the Patriots.

The game started out in familiar fashion, however, with the Patriots ahead. It started on a lucky bounce, when Brady fumbled a handoff near the goal line and the ball started rolling toward the end zone. Several Colts defenders had a chance to snatch up the fumble and end the drive, but instead it rolled through their hands and into the arms of New England guard Logan Mankins for a touchdown. It got worse from there, and before long Tony and his team found themselves trailing 21–3. Adding that to the fact that Brady and Belichick had never lost a conference championship made Indy's Super Bowl hopes seem pretty dim.

Tony refused to see it that way, however. He went to some of his players on the sideline and told them, "We're going to win this game."

It was a bold statement, but Tony believed in his players. The Colts added a field goal before halftime to cut the lead to 15 points. At halftime, Tony repeated himself, insisting that the Colts were going to win the game.

His confidence was well placed. The Colts came out and scored right away in the second half, cutting the lead to 21–13.

After a New England punt, they did it again. The six points for the touchdown left them down by 2 points. Tony had a decision to make: either go for the two-point conversion or kick the extra point. Many coaches are reluctant to go for two points until late in the game. After all, an extra point is almost automatic. But the Colts offense was running well, and Tony wanted to pull into a tie. So he called for the two-point try. Manning took the snap, dropped back, and calmly found Harrison for the conversion. In a little more than half a quarter, the Colts had come all the way back to tie the game at 21–21.

The Patriots weren't done, though. The teams traded several scores, resulting in a 34–31 New England lead. The Patriots had the ball with less than four minutes remaining in the fourth quarter. A first down would allow them to run off most of the remaining time, so the Colts defense had to step up. They did exactly that, forcing New England to punt the ball away with just over two minutes to go.

Manning brought the offense onto the field, knowing that they needed a field goal to tie or a touchdown to take the lead. The quarterback led the team deep into Patriots' territory with a series of pinpoint passes. The Colts were already well within field-goal range. Many coaches would have played it safe in that situation, but Tony and Manning went for the win. With about one minute to go, running back Joseph Addai ran in a 3-yard touchdown to give the Colts a 38–34 lead. The defense intercepted Brady on the Patriots' last, desperate drive, and it was over. Tony and the Colts had finally done it—they'd gotten past the Patriots! They were headed to the Super Bowl! The crowd went crazy as the players celebrated the big win. Confetti rained down on the field as Tony and Belichick shook hands at midfield.

"I'm so proud of the way our guys fought," Tony said. "I'm very happy for Peyton. He was very, very calm. He had to bring us from behind three or four times. It's just fitting. Our team went the hard way the whole year."

❝We have a great group of guys who are very unified. But I think God orchestrated this in such a way that we can't take credit for it. We just want to thank Him for giving us the strength to persevere.❞

—TONY AFTER THE COLTS' WIN
IN THE AFC CHAMPIONSHIP GAME

Indianapolis's opponent in the big game would be the Chicago Bears, coached by Lovie Smith. That was significant to Tony for several reasons. First, Smith had been an assistant coach with Tony in Tampa, so the two were great friends. Second, Smith was also an African American, meaning that for the first time in NFL history, two black head coaches would be squaring off in the Super Bowl.

For once, Tony didn't downplay the significance of his accomplishment. "It means a lot," he said. "I'm very proud of being an African American. I'm very proud of Lovie."

The two weeks leading up to the Super Bowl had a circus-like atmosphere. Reporters from around the globe came to Miami for Super Bowl XLI. Every angle of the game was analyzed and analyzed again. Most experts agreed that the Colts were by far the better team. The Bears had an excellent defense, but their offense, led by quarterback Rex Grossman, often struggled. In fact, Grossman was routinely booed by his own hometown fans. The wisdom of most experts was that if the Colts could limit their mistakes, there was no way the Bears could keep up with them.

Tony didn't want his players to be overconfident, however. He warned them that it wouldn't be easy. "Tomorrow night, there is going to be a storm in Dolphin Stadium," he said. "We might get off to a slow start and have to claw our way back, but we can do it. We will do it. . . . It is our time. Let's go win a championship."

Tony's words proved prophetic (and not just because of the pouring rain that fell on the stadium that day). The Bears won the coin toss and elected to receive the kickoff. Right away, Tony had a decision to make. The Bears' Devin Hester was one of the best return men the league had seen in years. Many teams refused to kick deep to him for fear of a big kickoff return. Coaches were willing to let the Chicago offense get the ball at the 30- or 40-yard line just to avoid Hester. But Tony decided against kicking short. He'd take his chances with Hester.

 Super Bowl XLI was the first Super Bowl in NFL history to be played in the rain.

It was a mistake he'd make only once that game. Hester fielded the kick near the sideline. He darted toward the middle of the field, putting on a dazzling series of moves and fakes that left the Colts' coverage team grasping at air. Hester and the Bears celebrated as he ran the ball into the end zone. Just like that, the Colts were down 7–0. It was exactly the sort of storm Tony had warned his players about.

And that wasn't the end of it. On offense, Manning was having a hard time gripping the wet football, leading to a Chicago interception deep in Indy territory. But the Colts' defense stepped up and prevented the Bears from scoring again. Then Manning and the offense went to work. They scored a touchdown but missed the extra point, to make the score 7–6. Chicago scored again to extend the lead to 8, but it was all Indy from that point on. The Colts' defense smothered Grossman and the Bears in the final three quarters, holding them to just 3 more points for the rest of the game. Manning wasn't as sharp as usual—largely because of the wet conditions—but he did more than enough to secure a 29–17 win and a Super Bowl championship.

❝*[Tony] is a man who has used his [fame] to behave in a quiet and strong way in the face of personal tragedy that has influenced a lot of our fellow citizens. And I want to thank you for your courage.***❞**
—PRESIDENT GEORGE W. BUSH CONGRATULATING TONY AND THE COLTS ON THEIR SUPER BOWL WIN

Would the big win be the end of Tony's coaching career? Many experts thought he might finally walk away now that he'd taken the Colts to the top. But he decided to come back.

"Every year, probably in the last three of four years, I've kind of evaluated where I am at the end of the year," he said. "I still have a lot of passion for the game, a lot of enthusiasm. After a night like [the Super Bowl], how can you not love it? I'm very fired up and looking forward to coming back."

Colts fans couldn't have been happier.

Tony's Legacy

Tony and the Colts followed up their championship with another good season in 2007. They started the season 7–0 before losing 24–20 to New England in a battle of unbeaten teams. The win marked a transfer of power in the AFC back to New England. (The Patriots went on to finish the season undefeated at 16–0.) The Colts never fully recovered and didn't look as strong later in the season. They finished with a good 13–3 mark, an AFC South title, and a first-round bye, however. NFL fans around the league anticipated a Patriots–Colts AFC Championship game—many of them believing that the meeting was all but assured. But it didn't work out that way. In the first round, Indy faced a San Diego Chargers team that was badly hampered by injury. In spite of that, the Chargers still managed to beat the Colts with a backup quarterback and a backup running back. The 28–24 loss left the Indianapolis crowd in stunned silence. The Colts would not get a chance to defend their Super Bowl title. They wouldn't even get a crack at the unbeaten Patriots in the AFC title game. The Patriots went on to win that game but lost in the Super Bowl to the Giants.

After the Colts lost to the Chargers in the playoffs, rumors again swirled about Tony retiring from coaching. But after a week of thinking, he decided to return to the Colts for the 2008 season.

It was another season of highs and lows for Tony and the Colts. The team stumbled out of the gate with a 3–4 record but finished strong, winning its last nine games of the year to finish 12–4. That mark was good enough to earn a Wild Card berth. The Colts were heavily favored to beat the Chargers, who had won the AFC West with an 8–8 record. But once again, San Diego sent the Colts home early, winning an overtime contest 23–17. As Tony walked off the field, everyone wondered whether he'd just coached his final game.

Tony told reporters he needed time to talk with his family and pray before he made up his mind. Then, about a week later, he announced that his coaching career was over. He was ready to devote more of his time to his family and to volunteering.

"These seven years have been better than I could ever have imagined," Tony said at a press conference. "[Lauren and I] just felt this was the right time. Don't shed any tears for me. I got to live a dream most people don't get to live."

Over 13 seasons as a head coach with the Bucs and Colts, Tony compiled a record of 139–69. His winning percentage of .668 ranks him seventh of all time among coaches with at least 100 games. His ten straight playoff appearances from 1999 through 2008 is an NFL record. At the relatively young age of 53, Tony would have had plenty of time to challenge more coaching records, but that's not what Tony cared about.

Tony Dungy came into the NFL in 1977, more than twenty years before the league would get its first black head coach. At that time, the thought of a black quarterback wasn't even something that most organizations took seriously. But his success as an assistant and then as a head coach was a big part in changing the way the NFL looked at African Americans in leadership roles. He was just the third black head coach in NFL history, and he became the first in league history to win a Super Bowl. His calm demeanor, deep knowledge of the game, and ability to relate to his players have made him one of the game's legendary coaches.

It hasn't always been an easy road for Tony, but hard work, perseverance, and dedication have made him a success both on and off the field. He's a role model and a hero to many, and his influence will resonate for decades to come.

PERSONAL STATISTICS

Name:

Anthony Kevin Dungy

Born:

October 6, 1955

College:

University of Minnesota

College Position:

Quarterback

NFL Position:

Safety

Height:

6 feet

Weight:

188 pounds

CAREER NFL STATISTICS

Defense

Year	Team	Games	Starts	Interceptions	Return Yards
1977	PIT	14	0	3	37
1978	PIT	16	2	6	95
1979	SF	15	7	0	0
Career		45	9	9	132

Offense

Year	Team	Pass Attempts	Pass Completions	Passing Yards	Rushes	Rushing Yards
1977	PIT	8	3	43	3	8

PIT, Pittsburgh Steelers; SF, San Francisco 49ers

Head-Coaching Record

Year	Team	W–L	Winning %	Playoff W–L
1996	TB	6–10	.375	0–0
1997	TB	10–6	.625	1–1
1998	TB	8–8	.500	0–0
1999	TB	11–5	.688	1–1
2000	TB	10–6	.625	0–1
2001	TB	9–7	.563	0–1
2002	IND	10–6	.625	0–1
2003	IND	12–4	.750	2–1
2004	IND	12–4	.750	1–1
2005	IND	14–2	.875	0–1
2006	IND	12–4	.750	4–0
2007	IND	13–3	.813	0–1
2008	IND	12–4	.750	0-1
CAREER	13 seasons	139–69	.668	9–10

TB, Tampa Bay Buccaneers; IND, Indianapolis Colts

GLOSSARY

autobiography: a book someone writes about his or her own life

blitz: a defensive play in which defenders who don't usually rush the quarterback do so

draft: a system for selecting new players for professional sports teams

pocket: the protected area behind a team's offensive line, from which the quarterback usually throws or hands off the ball

rookie: a first-year player

scholarship: money given to a student to help pay the costs of schooling

strike: a walkout by a group of workers. Workers strike in an attempt to get higher wages, better working conditions, or more benefits.

Tampa 2: a form of the "cover 2" defense that focuses on preventing long plays and getting turnovers (also called the Minnesota Cover 2)

Wild Card: a team that earns a playoff spot despite not winning its division. The NFL awards Wild Card spots to the top two non-division winners in each conference.

SOURCES

1 Tom Powers, "Dungy Exhibits the Product of Preparation, Desperation," *St. Paul Pioneer Press*, October 14, 1996.

3 Sid Hartman, "Jubilant Dungy Basks in Success," *Star Tribune*, October 14, 1996.

4–5 Tony Dungy, *Quiet Strength* (Carol Stream, IL: Tyndale House, 2007), 8.

7 Jarrett Bell, "Dungy's Upbringing Was Super Solid," *USA Today*, January 30, 2007, http://www.usatoday.com/sports/football/nfl/colts/2007-01-29-dungy-cover_x.htm.

7 Bell, "Dungy's Upbringing."

8 Ibid.

9 Joel A. Rippel, *Game of My Life, Minnesota: Memorable Stories of Gopher Football* (Champaign, IL, Sports Publishing, 2007), 107.

10 Dungy, *Quiet Strength*, 29.

12 Terry Cullen, "Cornhuskers Dominate Gopher Pass Defense in Easy Triumph," *Minnesota Daily*, October 8, 1973.

12 Terry Cullen, "Gopher Gridders Spoil Hawkeyes Homecoming," *Minnesota Daily*, October 22, 1973.

13 Rippel, *A Game of My Life*, 108.

14 Terry Cullen, "Quarterback's Hard Knocks Don't Dent Improved Attitude," *Minnesota Daily*, October 16, 1973.

14 Terry Cullen, "'Rudder' Dungy Steers Gopher Offense Toward Full Sail," *Minnesota Daily*, September 24, 1974.

14 Rippel, *A Game of My Life*, 108.

15 Bob Fowler, "Gophers Win Respect While Losing to Buckeyes," *Minneapolis Star*, September 16, 1974.

16 Terry Cullen, "Gophers Keep Bronze Pig Floyd by Defeating Iowa Hawkeyes 23-17," *Minnesota Daily*, October 21, 1974.

17 Dungy, *Quiet Strength*, 30.

18 Marty Duda, "Gophers' Victory Primer for Big Ten Games," *Minnesota Daily*, October 6, 1975.

19 Craig Thompson, "Gophers 'Pass' Test against Wolverine 'Big Boys,' *Minnesota Daily*, November 3, 1975.

19 Christina Verderosa, "Dungy, Kullas Set Aerial Records in Win over Northwestern," *Minnesota Daily*, November 10, 1975.

20 Craig Thompson, "Stoll Re-examines Northwestern Game, Anticipates Ohio Contest," *Minnesota Daily*, November 11, 1975.

20 Craig Thompson, "Gopher Performance Poor in Mistake-Filled Loss to Powerful Buckeye Team," *Minnesota Daily*, November 17, 1975.

22 University of Minnesota Athletics Department, Special for Metro College Publications, Interview Story with Tony Dungy, Gopher QB (press release), n.d.

23 Bob Fowler, "Slater at Center of Gophers Win," *Minneapolis Star*, September 13, 1976.

23 University of Minnesota Athletics Department, Interview.

23 Bob Fowler, "Gophers Need Depth More Than Rout," *Minneapolis Star*, September 20, 1976.

24 Tom Mason, "Gophers Stumble on Way to Late 21–10 Gridiron Triumph," *Minnesota Daily*, September 27, 1976.

24 Tom Mason, "52,606 Homecoming Fans Look On as Gophers French Fry Illini 29-14," *Minnesota Daily*, October 11, 1976.

25 Rippel, *A Game of My Life*, 111.

25 Mason, "52,606 Homecoming Fans."

27 University of Minnesota Athletics Department, Interview.

29 Dungy, *Quiet Strength*, 36.

30 Ibid., 37.

31 Ibid., 38.

34 Ibid., 48.

35 Ibid., 51.

36 Jim Wexell, *Tales from Behind the Steel Curtain* (Champaign, IL: Sports Publishing, 2004), 84.

39 Wexell, *Tales*, 13.

41 Dungy, *Quiet Strength*, 68.

43 Thomas George, "Leading the Chiefs on Upward Climb," *New York Times*, December 16, 1990, http://query.nytimes.com/gst/fullpage.html?res=9C0CE5DA173EF935A25751C1A966958260.

45–46 Thomas George, "Defenses Are Putting the Ball in Their Courts," *New York Times*, December 31, 1992, http://query.nytimes.com/gst/fullpage.html?res=9E0CE2DB1539F932A05751C1A964958260.

47 Mike Freeman, "Vikings' Defensive Coordinator Is Too Busy to Take Calls," *New York Times*, January 1, 1995, http://query.nytimes.com/gst/fullpage.html?res=990CE6D61E30F932A35752C0A963958260.

50 Dungy, *Quiet Strength*, 120.

51 Ibid., ii.

53 Ibid., 132.

54 Charean Williams, "Dilfer, Bucs Elated to Be Home for Holidays," *Chicago Tribune*, December 22, 1997.

55 Thomas George, "Bucs' Playoff Novices Check Sanders and Deck the Lions," *New York Times*, December 29, 1997.

55 George, "Playoff Novices."

57 John Mullin, "Word Is Out: Bears Vanish in 2nd Halves," *Chicago Tribune*, September 21, 1998.

60 Pete Williams, "There's No Quit in This Ballclub," *Washington Post*, January 16, 2000.

62 Bill Pennington, "Tampa Bay Lets Secret Slip Away at Wrong Time," *New York Times*, January 24, 2000.

63 Chris Harrys and Joey Johnston, *Tales from the Bucs Sideline* (Champaign, IL: Sports Publishing, 2004), 147.

67 Ibid., 155.

68 Dungy, *Quiet Strength*, 203.

69 Harry, *Tales from the Bucs*, 159.

69 Damon Hack, "FOOTBALL: Manning and Dungy a Not-So-Odd Couple," *New York Times*, July 25, 2002, http://query.nytimes.com/gst/fullpage.html?res=9D04E6D91038F936A15754C0A9649C8B63.

70 Mike Chappell and Phil Richards, *Tales from the Indianapolis Colts Sideline* (Champaign, IL: Sports Publishing, 2004), 68.

72 Dungy, *Quiet Strength*, 212.

74 Ibid., 222.

75 Associated Press, "Bucs' Defense Allows 28 2nd-half Points," *ESPN.com*, October 6, 2003, http://sports.espn.go.com/nfl/recap?gameId=231006027.

76 "Manning was 22-of-26 for 377 yards, 5 TDs," *ESPN.com*, January 4, 2004, http://sports.espn.go.com/nfl/recap?gameId=240104011.

76 John Clayton, "Smith, Dungy Will Make This a Classy Super Bowl," *ESPN.com*, January 22, 2007, http://sports.espn.go.com/nfl/playoffs06/columns/story?columnist=clayton_john&id=2738645.

77 *ESPN*, "Law Nabs Three INTs, Vinatieri Boots Five FGs," *ESPN.com*, January 18, 2004, http://sports.espn.go.com/nfl/recap?gameId=240118017.

79 Associated Press, "New England Curse: Manning Falls to 0-7 in Foxboro," *ESPN.com*, January 16, 2005, http://sports.espn.go.com/nfl/recap?gameId=250116017.

81 Dungy, *Quiet Strength*, 244.

82 Associated Press, "Dungy Uncertain Whether He'll Rest Colts Starters," *ESPN.com*, December 6, 2005, http://sports.espn.go.com/nfl/news/story?id=2249945.

83 Dungy, *Quiet Strength*, 254.

83 Karen Crouse, "A Gentle Touch Develops Into a Winning One," *New York Times*, January 28, 2007, http://www.nytimes.com/2007/01/28/sports/football/28dungy.html.

85 Don Banks, "Are the Colts and Pats Still Super Bowl Contenders?" *SI.com*, December 10, 2006, http://sportsillustrated.cnn.com/2006/writers/don_banks/12/10/snap.judgments1/index.html.

86 NFL, "Jags Run away from Colts, Win 44-17," *NFL.com*, December 10, 2006, http://www.nfl.com/gamecenter/recap?game_id=29059.

87 Dungy, *Quiet Strength*, 284.

89 Associated Press, "Manning Finally Wins Big One, Leads Colts to Super Bowl," *ESPN.com*, January 21, 2007, http://sports-att.espn.go.com/nfl/recap?gameId=270121011.

89 Dungy, *Quiet Strength*, 288.

90 Associated Press, "Smith, Dungy Are First Black Coaches in Super Bowl," *ESPN.com*, January 22, 2007, http://sports.espn.go.com/nfl/playoffs06/news/story?id=2738495.

90 Dungy, *Quiet Strength*, 290.

92 Jeff Zillgitt, "All-class Dungy May Heed Greater Calling," *USA Today*, February 6, 2007, http://www.usatoday.com/sports/columnist/zillgitt/2007-02-06-zillgitt-dungy_x.htm.

92 White House Press Release, "President Bush Congratulates NFL Super Bowl Champion Indianapolis Colts," April 23, 2007, http://www.whitehouse.gov/news/releases/2007/04/20070423-6.html.

94–95 AP, "Dungy Retires after 7 Seasons with Colts," *ESPN.com*, January 12, 2009, http://sports.espn.go.com/nfl/news/story?id=3827058.

BIBLIOGRAPHY

Chappell, Mike, and Phil Richards. *Tales from the Indianapolis Colts Sideline*. Champaign, IL: Sports Publishing, 2004.

Dungy, Tony. *Quiet Strength: The Principles, Practices, and Priorities of a Winning Life*. Carol Stream, IL: Tyndale House, 2007.

Harry, Chris, and Joey Johnston. *Tales from the Bucs Sideline*. Champaign, IL: Sports Publishing, 2004.

Rippel, Joel A. *Game of My Life: Memorable Stories of Gophers Football*. Champaign, IL: Sports Publishing, 2007.

Wexell, Jim. *Tales from Behind the Steel Curtain*. Champaign, IL: Sports Publishing, 2004.

WEBSITES

Colts.com

http://www.colts.com

The official home page of the Indianapolis Colts includes all the latest team news and statistics, with photos, videos, and more.

NFL.com—The Official Site of the National Football League

http://www.nfl.com

The NFL's official site includes scores, news, statistics, video features, and other information for football fans.

Pro Football Reference—Tony Dungy

http://www.pro-football-reference.com/players/D/DungTo20.htm

Tony's page on this popular reference site includes his complete NFL playing statistics as well as his record as a head coach.

Tony Dungy—*Quiet Strength*

http://www.coachdungy.com

This site, which promotes Tony's autobiography, Quiet Strength, *includes information on the book and on Tony's life, a photo gallery, and more.*

INDEX